The Robin Wood Tarot Meditation and Coloring Book

By Robin Wood

The Robin Wood Tarot Meditation and Coloring Book

A Livingtree Book

April 2017

ISBN 0-9652984-4-2

Book Design by Robin Wood

For information, or to obtain permission, contact the author at:

Robin Wood
3319 Greenfield Rd. #102
Dearborn, MI 48120

Or visit the website at

http://robinwood.com

You can also follow Robin on Twitter @RobinWood

About this Coloring Book

Hi, and welcome to the Robin Wood Tarot Meditation Coloring Book!

When I made the Robin Wood Tarot, I started with pencil sketches, which I inked before I colored them in. This book has all those inked drawings, just the way they were when I colored them, although they are the size of the actual cards. (I colored them at four times the size, because Llewellyn insisted.)

At the top of each page, you'll find the name of the card, the Key from my book about the deck, and the meaning and reversed meaning from the little deck booklet that my husband, Michael Short, wrote.

Each card is on a right hand page, with the left hand page next to it left blank. That's so you can cut out the card, if you want to, and not destroy anything. You can also use that blank page for notes, so you can remind yourself about why you chose to use certain colors, or write down any epiphanies you have while coloring the cards. (If you intend to cut the cards out, you might want to keep the notes in a different place.)

Sadly, I'm not aware of any good way to have this book printed on card stock, so the cards will be too thin to shuffle. There are a couple of ways to fix that. One is to buy a blank deck. There are several available, and you can glue the colored cards to them, to make a deck you can actually use.

The second way is to copy the cards onto card stock before (or after) you color them.

I give you permission to copy the deck, as many times as needed, for your own personal use. Please don't sell them, or give out copies to non-family members. (Kids, spouses, siblings and parents are fine; but let others buy their own, please.) You can enlarge or shrink them while copying, if you want to, for use as decorations, or anything else you need to use them for. Or cut the figures out, and use them as paper dolls! Pretty much anything you like, as long as you don't give copies away, or sell them, without getting permission from me.

Mostly, I'm making this book available for those who want to really get into the deck, by coloring their own copies. When you do the coloring yourself, you might notice things about the cards that you never saw before.

Don't be limited by the colors I used on the deck, or by the drawings I did. Feel free to use colors that are meaningful to you, and to fill blank areas with your own designs. Let your imagination free as you color, and think about the meanings and symbols on each card, to make the deck your own.

Have fun with it!

Bright Blessings!

Robin Wood

About the Tarot

A traditional Tarot Deck has 78 cards, divided into 22 Major Arcana and 56 Minor Arcana cards.

The Major Arcana cards are the Greater Secrets, or Trumps, and are numbered 0 through 21. Each has a name, as well (The Fool, The Magician, etc.) They are what Jung would have called Archetypes, representing images and patterns which form the roots of everything else. In a reading, they symbolize forces the Seeker has no control over.

The Minor Arcana is divided into four suits, Pentacles, Swords, Wands and Cups, which each have a King, Queen, Knight, Page, and ten "pip" cards numbered 1 through 10.

The Pentacles are traditionally associated with the classical element of Earth, with quiet strength, rest, and peace, as well as richness, wisdom, and sensuality. The direction of the Pentacles is North, and the time is Midnight. Most of the people in this deck are alone, engaging in quiet, restful, creative pursuits. They are gaining knowledge, which requires some solitude to absorb the lessons learned elsewhere, distilling them into wisdom. Traditionally, the people in this suit have dark hair and eyes, which I tried to reflect when I colored the deck, but you certainly don't have to when you color yours, unless you find meaning there.

The Swords are one of the two suits that are associated with Air in some decks, and Fire in others. (The other is Wands.) I was aware of this when I drew the cards, and thought about it for a while before I chose to associate Swords with Air in my deck. I eventually went this direction because of a bunch of reasons, but the central one was that this suit is associated with knowledge, which is sharp, and cuts both ways.

Which meant that Wands would be associated with Fire. Some of my friends were very unhappy that I chose the way I did, and explained that Fire would burn up the wands. I had thought that was part of the point; the wands were fuel for the fire. But the more I thought, the more I realized they were much more than that; Fire is associated with willpower, and wands are used to channel the will. That's why I made them magic wands, and most I saw as metal. You can color them all as if they are made of wood if you want, though!

So, in this deck, Swords are associated with Air, with action, courage, trouble, authority, health and gathering knowledge, which can be a very painful pursuit. Their direction is the East, their time, Morning. The cards of this suit deal with sacrifice, redemption, and transformation. Traditionally, the people here are those with dark hair and light eyes.

Wands are associated with Fire, with growth, will, business, negotiations, family, and nimble speech. Their direction is South, their time is Noon. The cards here deal with struggle, focusing the will, self-control, creativity, and using energy wisely. The people on these cards traditionally have blond or red hair, and light eyes.

Finally, the suit of Cups is associated with Water, and with the whole range of emotional matters; friendship, love, contentment, soul-searching, and discontent, as well as imagination, dreams and healing. The direction is West, the time is Evening. This suit is all about handling emotions, from healing friendship and love to disillusionment and despair, from aspirations, dreams and fantasies to longing and abandonment. Everything that comes from the heart, and flows like the tides. The people on these cards have light hair and eyes.

I've arranged the cards in the order listed above; Majors first, then the Pentacles, Swords, Wands and Cups from highest to lowest. Ace, King, Queen, Knight, Page, then 10 through 2. This is the way they're arranged in the little booklet that comes with my deck, and after some discussion, I decided to keep that order.

I have also decided not to try to tell you how to use the deck in this book. This is for meditation, after all. If you don't know how to read the cards, I have some information about that on my website, at http://robinwood.com/LivingtreeGrove/Tarot/TarotSet.html

I have also written a book about my deck, specifically, which tells you more about the symbols I chose, and why I chose them, and also has a section about reading the cards, the history of the Tarot, and a short section about how to play Tarocchi, which is the game the deck was invented for. You can find that on my site at http://robinwood.com/Catalog/Books/BookPages/RWTDeck.html if you're interested. (I also have it on Amazon, in both print and Kindle editions.)

And, of course, there are dozens and dozens of other books that will tell you how to read, and what the cards are all about, as well.

Notes:

0 The Fool

Key - Pay Attention

Meaning - Thoughtlessness, folly, lightheartdness, innocence. Purity of heart. Lack of discipline. One seeking fulfillment and experience. Freedom, lack of restraint.

Reversed - Carelessness, vanity, indecision, apathy, poor judgement. Lack of control.

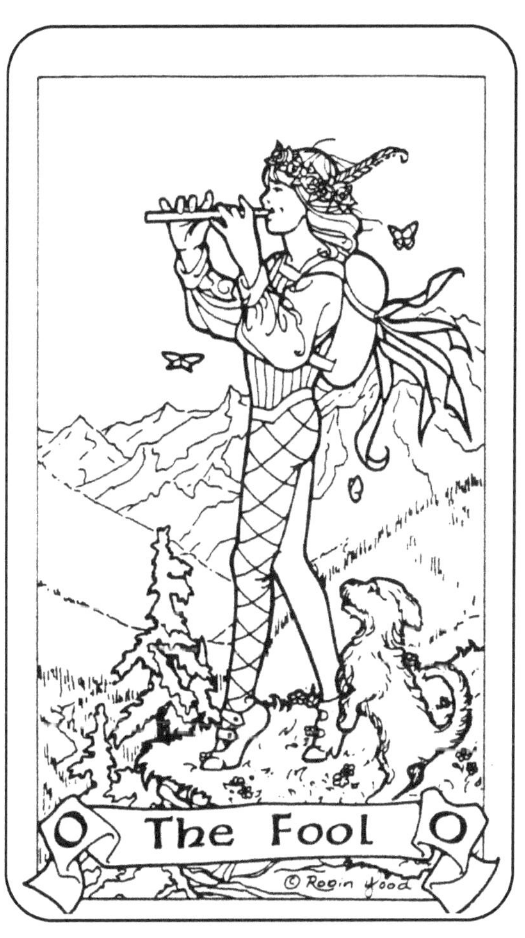

Notes:

1 - The Magician

Key - Creativity

Meaning - Opportunities to use talents. Originality, creativity, imagination, skill, diplomacy, self-reliance. The merging of the four elements.

Reversed - Unskilled, clumsy, insecure, disgrace, bad judgement causes loss.

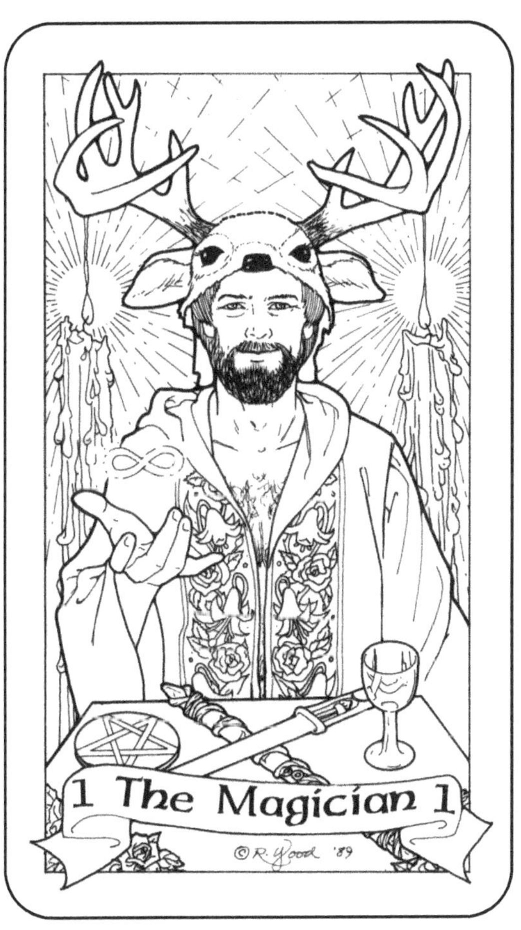

Notes:

2 - *The High Priestess*

Key - Wisdom and Compassion

Meaning - Practicality, good judgement, wisdom, mystery, the clouded future. A woman of interest to the Seeker, or the Seeker herself.

Reversed - Passion, conceit, lack of sense, poor intuition, ignorance, bad judgement.

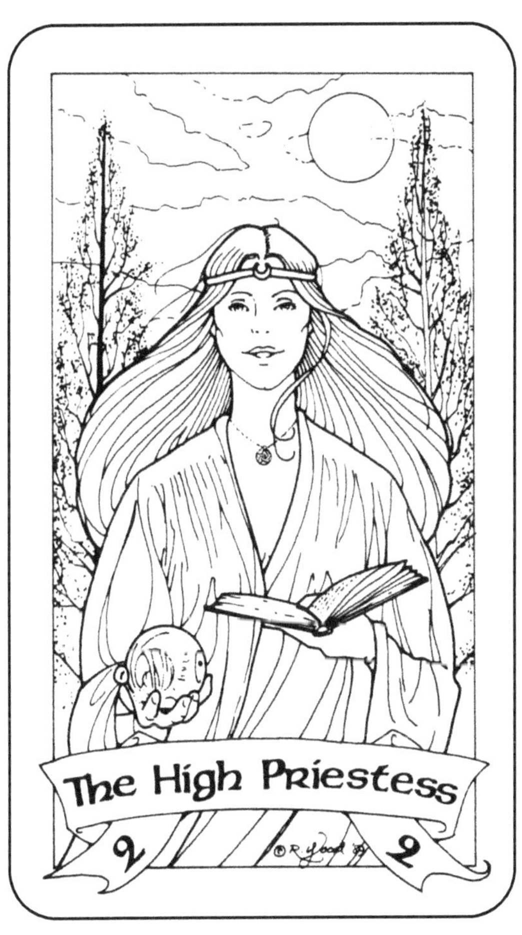

Notes:

3 - The Empress

Key - Mother

Meaning - Pregnancy, fertility, good advice, safety, security, hidden actions. A competent woman, safe and secure, who is building a future for herself and her family.

Reversed - Lack of satisfaction. The unraveling of involved matters. Uncertainty, infidelity, infertility.

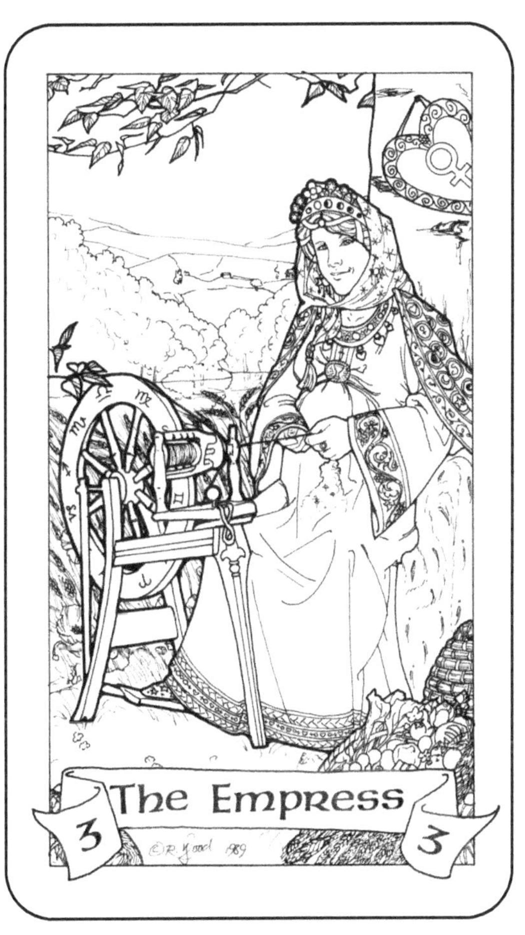

Notes:

4 - The Emperor

Key - Father

Meaning - A father figure, secure and successful. A stable, authoritative, powerful leader. A person with the qualities of reason and conviction.

Reversed - Confusion, obstruction, immaturity, ineffectiveness, weakness of character, megalomania.

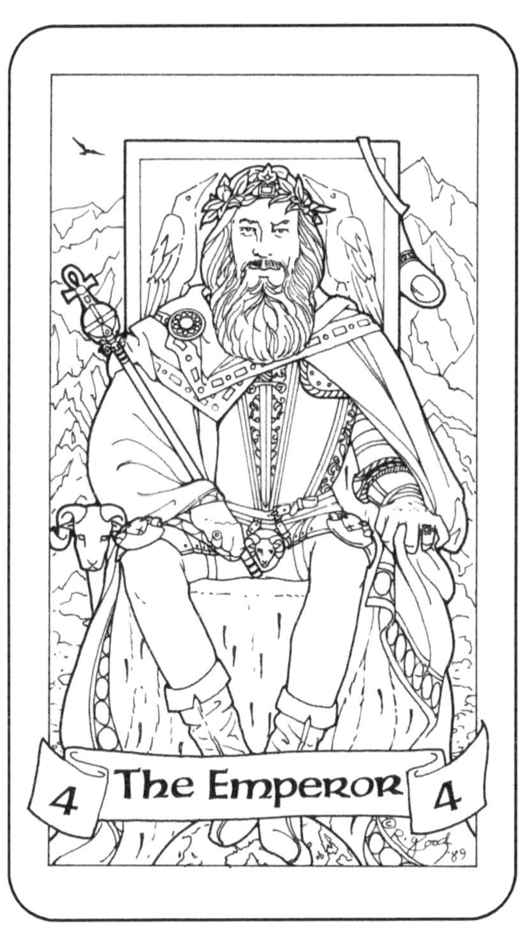

Notes:

5 - The Hierophant

Key - Conformity

Meaning - Tradition, captivity, servitude, ritual, inactivity, retention, timidity. A desire to hold on to old thoughts and ways even if they are outdated. Concern for form over function.

Reversed - A foolish exercise in generosity, eccentricity, intrigue, weakness.

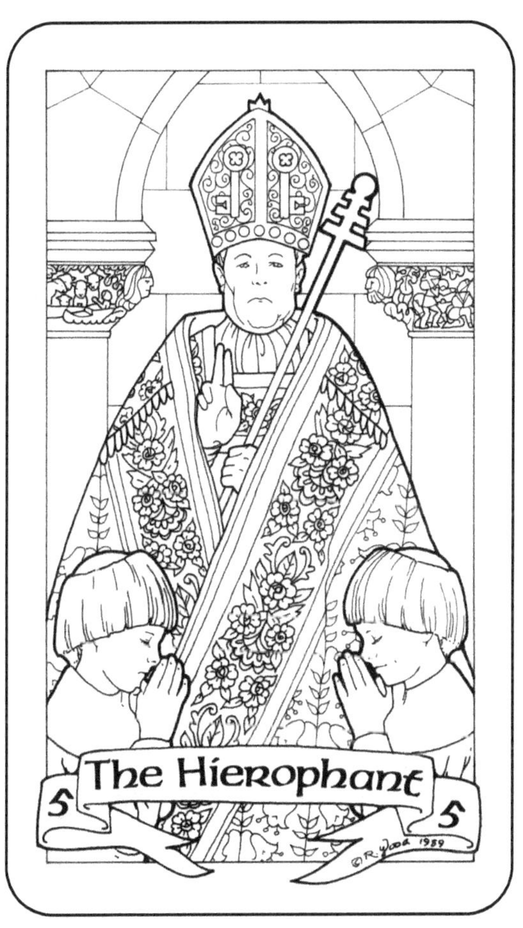

Notes:

6 - The Lovers

Key - Love and companionship

Meaning - Love, respect, partnership, trust, communication, perfection, honor, romance, beauty. A couple which has worked together to overcome trials.

Reversed - Failure, unreliability, separation, frustration in marriage, instability, confusion, silence. The inability or disinclination to share thoughts.

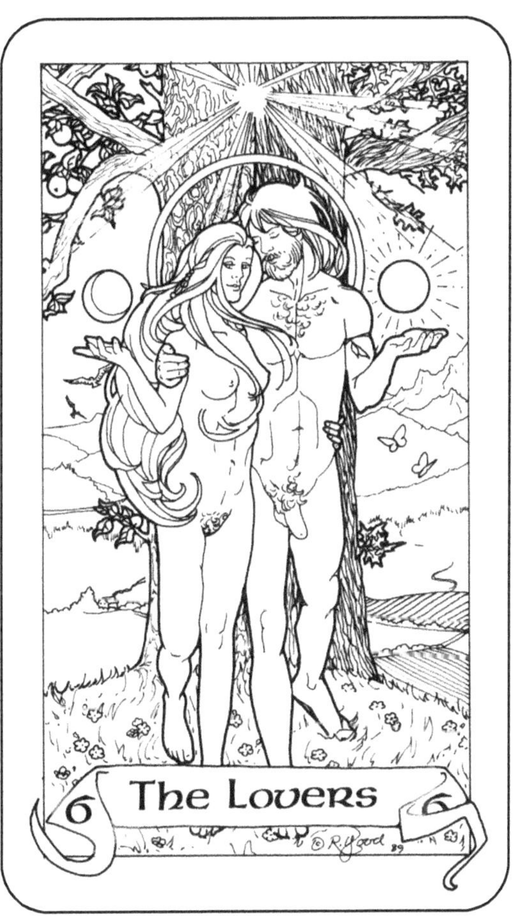

Notes:

7 - *The Chariot*

Key - Balance and Harmony

Meaning - Work and travel, purpose, trouble or problems fall behind, triumph, harmony, balance. Controlling forces which might conflict and bringing them together to form a working whole.

Reversed - Quarrels, trouble, defeat, failure, the collapse of hopes or dreams, unfavorable legal proceedings.

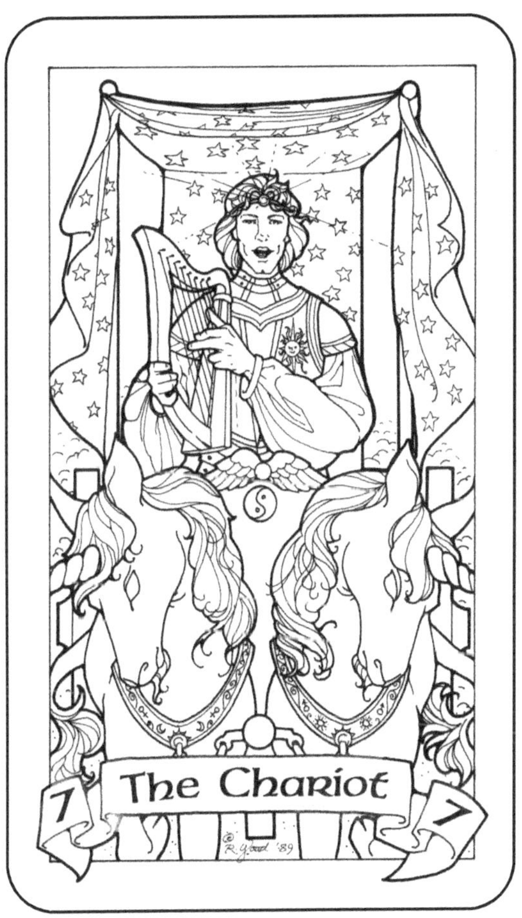

Notes:

8 - Strength

Key - Strength of Spirit

Meaning - Power, energy, strength, courage, conviction. The gift to sooth others' grief or help solve their problems.

Reversed - Weakness, sickness, lack of faith, despotism, discord, abuse of power, a fear of loneliness.

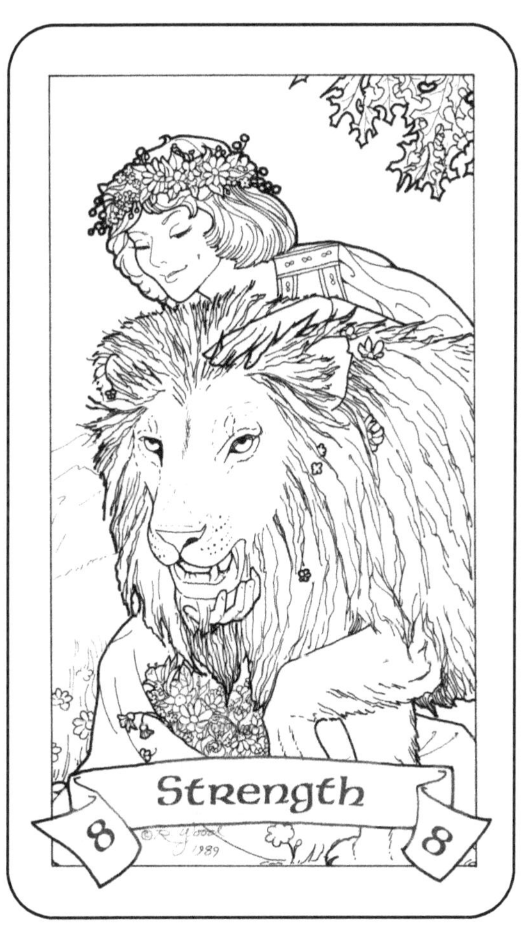

Notes:

9 - The Hermit

Key - Meditation and Contemplation

Meaning - Meditation, the search for truth, good counsel, wisdom, prudence. A withdrawal from life is needed to find one's center.

Reversed - Hastiness, imprudence, unreasoning caution or fear, emotional immaturity. Withdrawal from one's problems with no constructive plans.

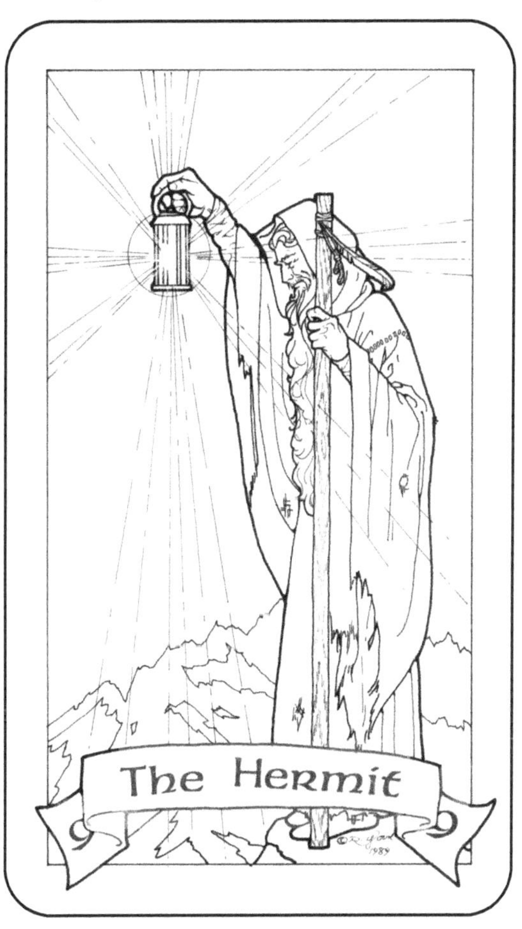

Notes:

10 - Wheel of Fortune

Key - Roller Coaster Ride

Meaning - Change, destiny, fortune, good luck, the end of troubles in sight. Moving ahead for better or worse.

Reversed - Reversal of fortunes, failure, bad luck, unexpected interference.

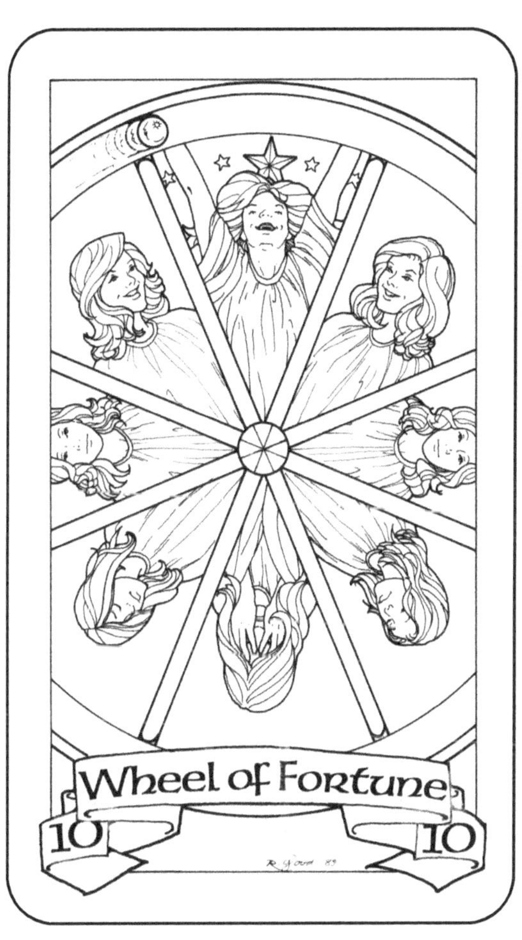

Notes:

11 - Justice

Key - Fairness

Meaning - Fairness, balance, equality, rightness, legal matters, negotiations.

Reversed - Bias, prejudice, bigotry, intolerance, a bad legal decision, cruel punishment.

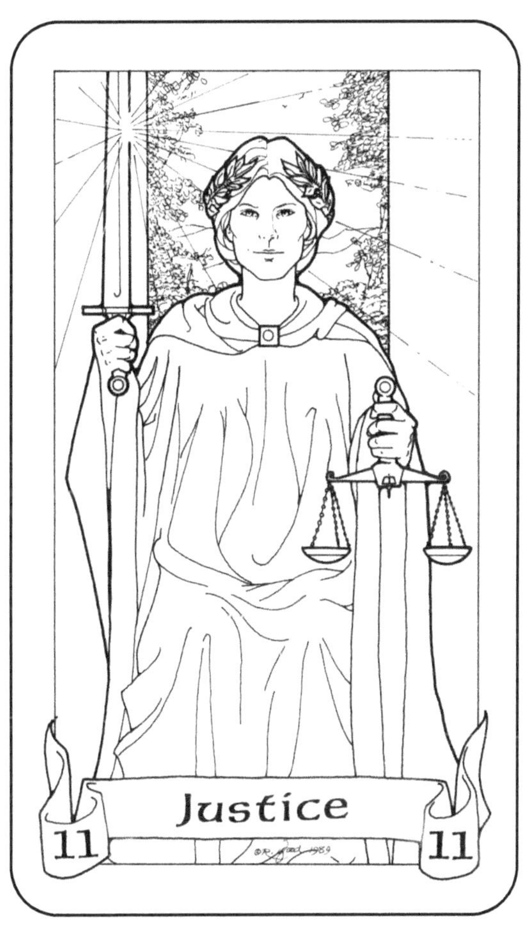

Notes:

12 - The Hanged Man

Key - New Point of View

Meaning - Suspense, life interrupted, change. Wisdom in occult matters. Sacrifice for wisdom. Inner search for truth. Change in your point of view.

Reversed - A wasteful search, selfishness. Lack of effort needed to achieve a goal. A useless gesture.

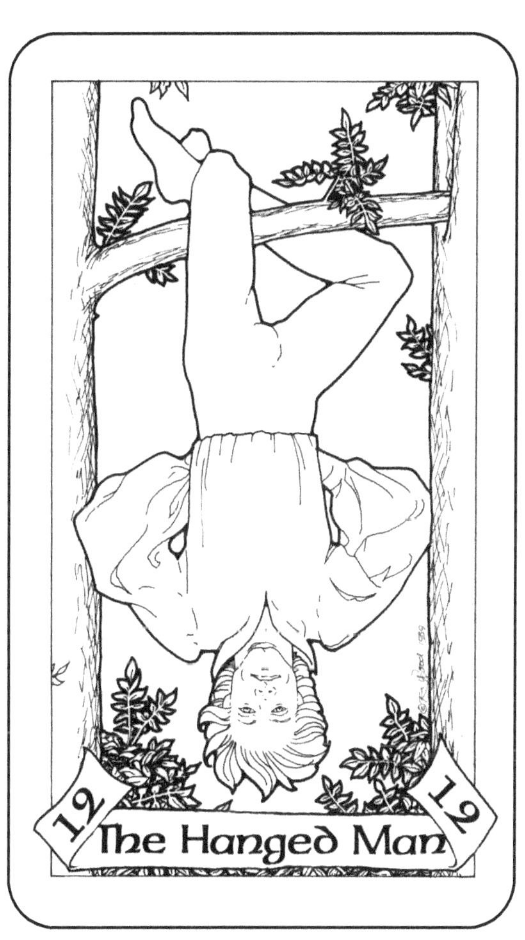

Notes:

13 - Death

Key - And Now, for Something Completely Different

Meaning - The end of an era (and the beginning of another.) A reminder of mortality. A great change. A discovery which changes the Seeker's life direction.

Reversed - Lethargy, great inertia, slow or ponderous change, depression. Resisting the inevitable.

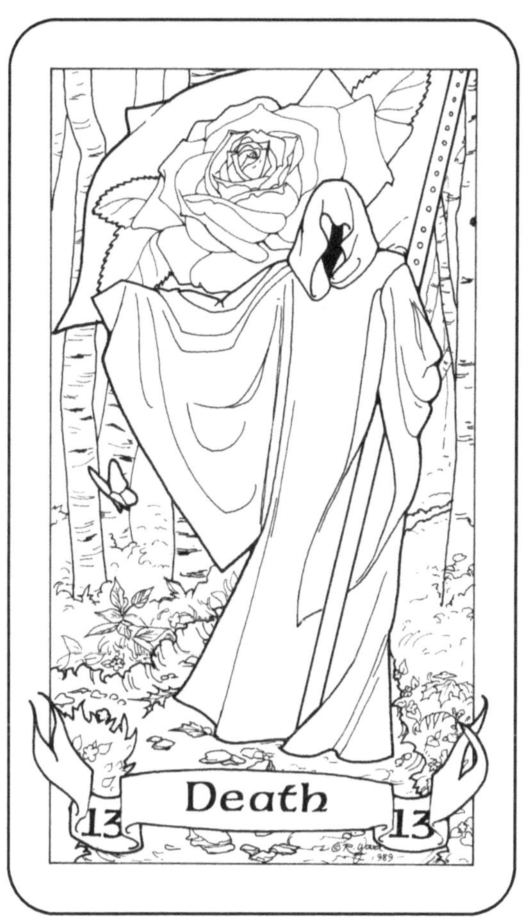

Notes:

MAJORS

14 - Temperance

Key - Moderation

Meaning - Economy, a moderate lifestyle, patience. Obtaining security through frugal management of means. Meditation. All things in moderation (including moderation!)

Reversed - Competitive interests. Too much caution. Hostility. A person it's impossible to work with. Misunderstanding others.

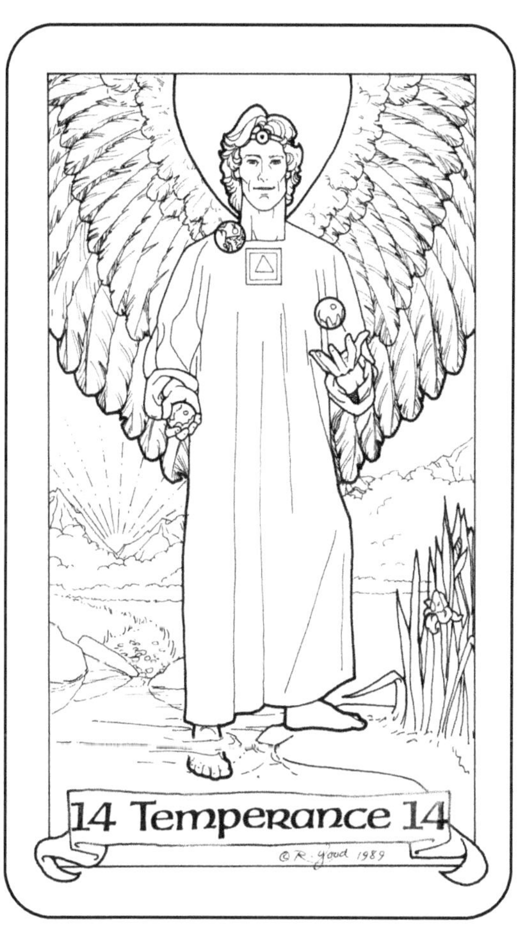

Notes:

15 - The Devil

Key - Greed

Meaning - Greed, the monkey trap. Vehement desires, lust. Bondage to an ideal. Bad or evil influence or advice. A choice upon which your fate depends. Dissolution.

Reversed - A release from bondage. A rest. A new life direction.

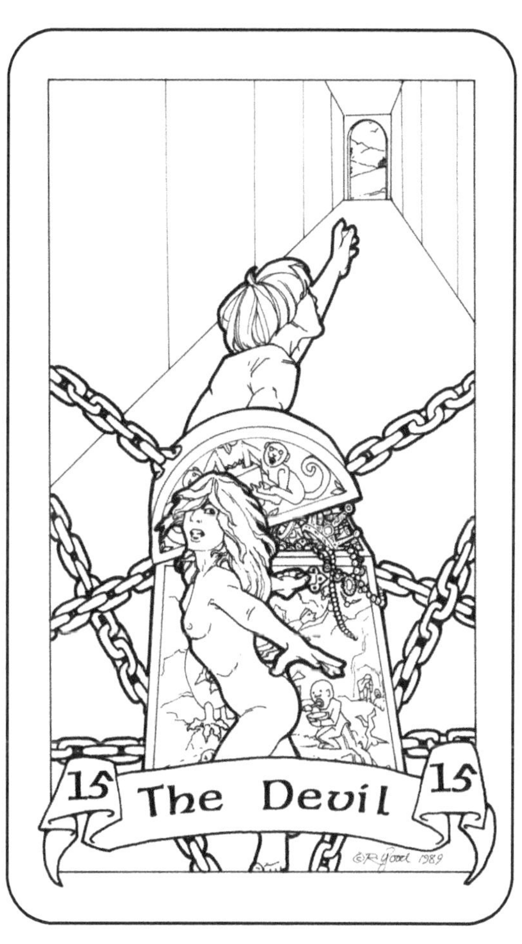

Notes:

16 - The Tower

Key - Now to Lose the False Premises

Meaning - Sudden change, broken friendships, destruction, security lost, disgrace. Catastrophic transformation.

Reversed - Tyranny, continued oppression. Lack of change, monetary losses.

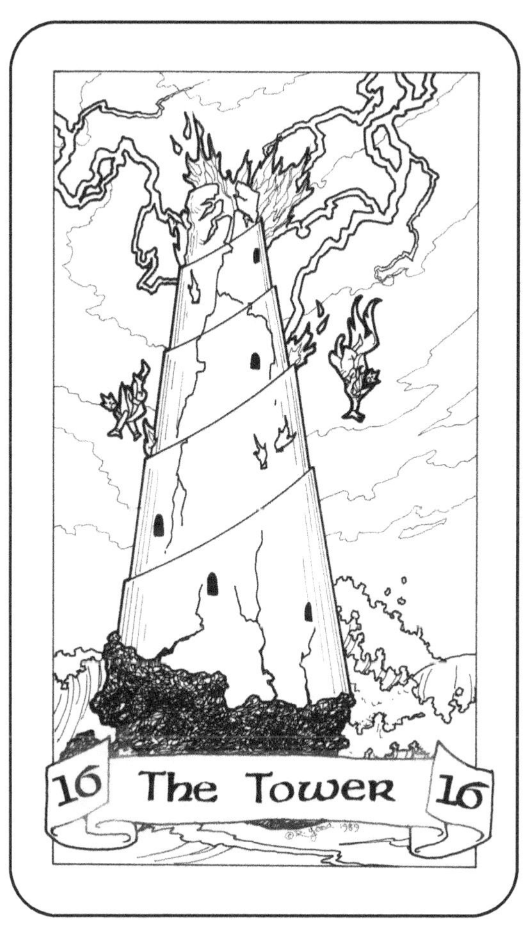

Notes:

17 - The Star

Key - Starlight Vision

Meaning - Hope and faith. A blending of the best of the past and present. Bright prospects. Mastering the occult arts. An awareness of two worlds.

Reversed - Laziness and indifference. Unrealized hopes. Arrogance, pride. Delays, loss of hope or faith.

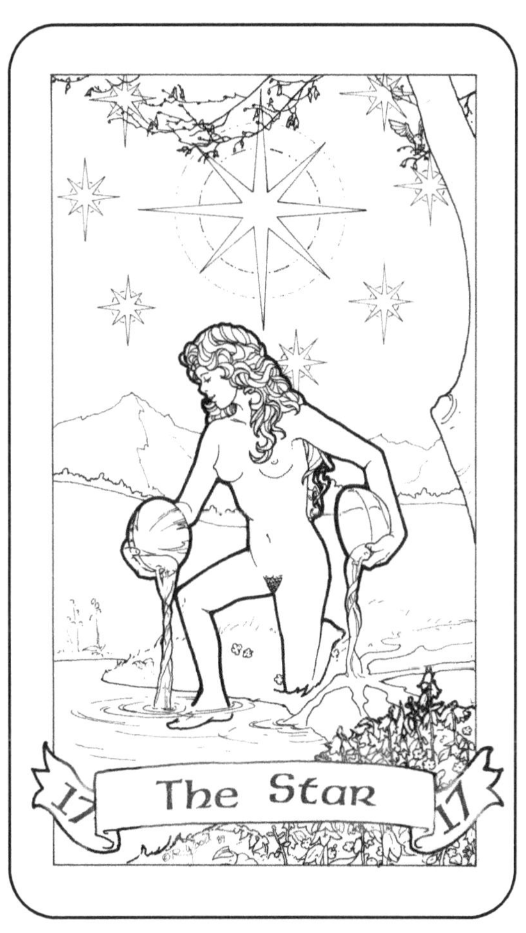

Notes:

18 - *The Moon*

Key - Wildness

Meaning - A warning, deception. Enemies who are out of sight. A caution to stay on your path for safety. Darkness, companions out of their element.

Reversed - A white lie, a trick, a tiny mistake. Silence, stillness. Unexpected gain with no cost exacted.

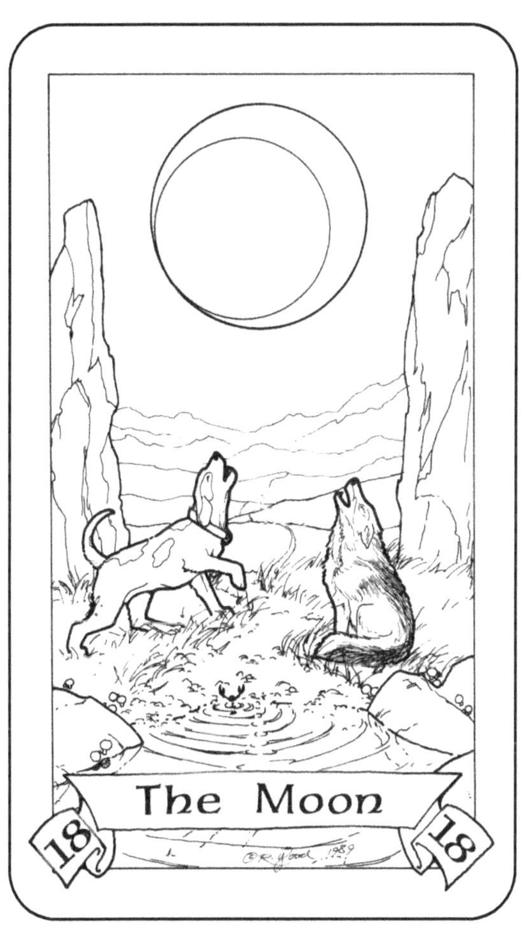

Notes:

19 - The Sun

Key - Joy

Meaning - Accomplishment, success, material happiness. A good marriage, joy, pleasure. Liberation, freedom, contentment.

Reversed - Lesser joys. A separation from loved ones. Delayed success or postponed security. An uncertain future.

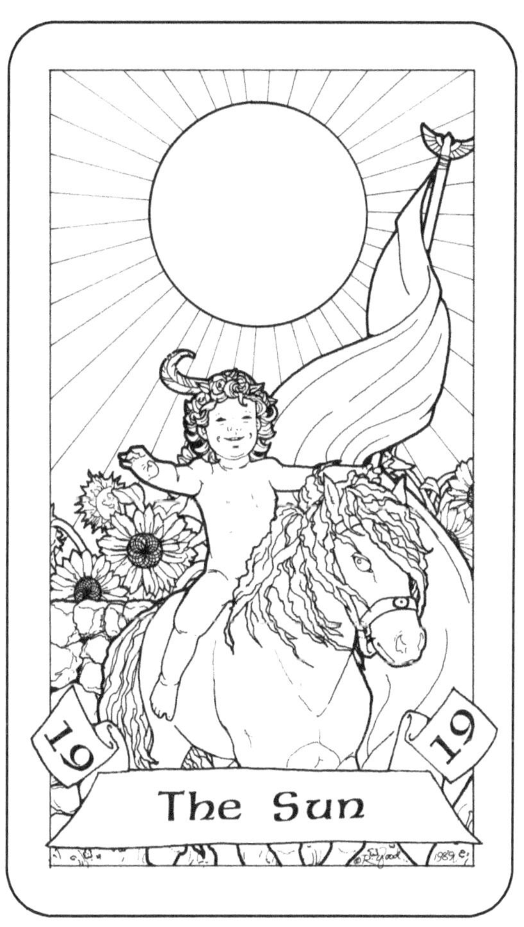

Notes:

20 - Judgement

Key - Rebirth

Meaning - A change of position, rejuvenation, rebirth. Reward, acquiring a purpose. Atonement, paying the piper, accounting for one's actions.

Reversed - Weakness. Lost affections, separation, divorce. Confrontation, indecision. Avoidance of obligations.

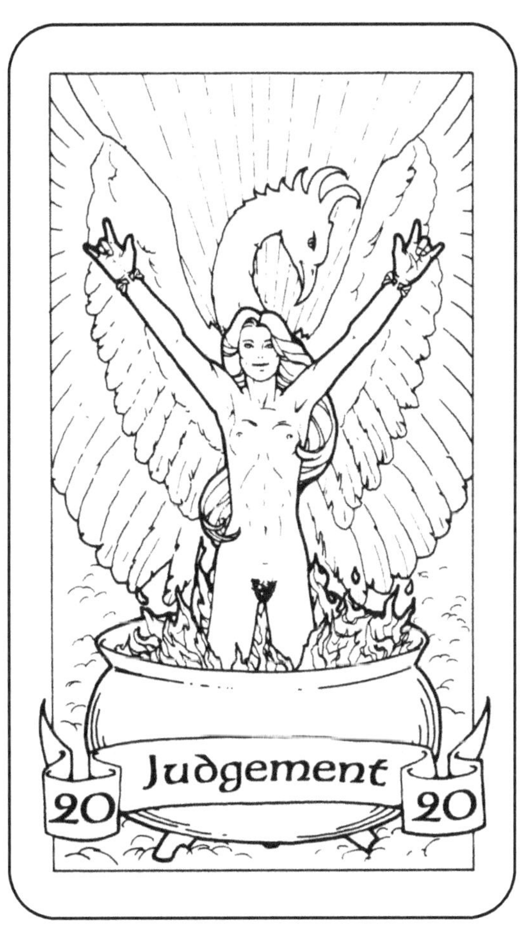

Notes:

21 - The World

Key - Wholeness and Mastery

Meaning - Completion, the end of a way of life, success. A new beginning, change of location, hope for the future. Triumph in the end. The admiration of friends. The breadth of possibilities.

Reversed - Disappointment. A discouragingly small advance. Failure, the inability to finish what you've started. Permanence, stagnation.

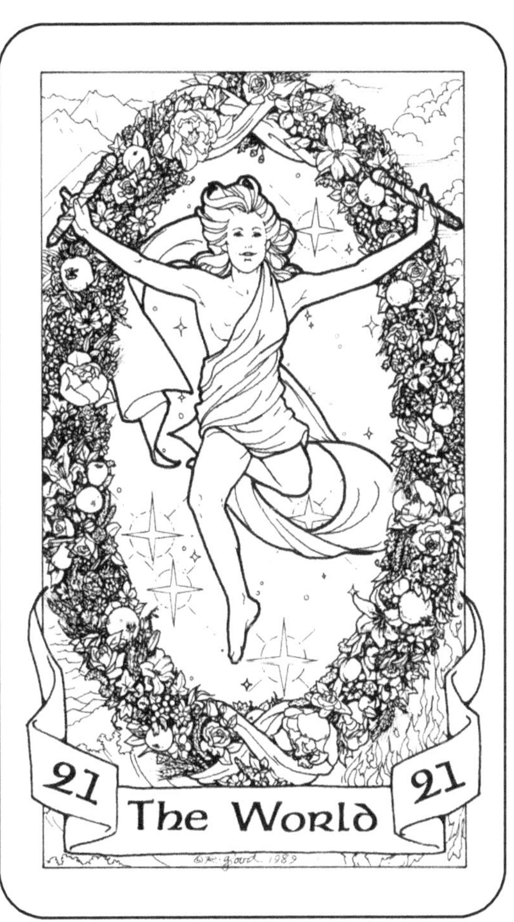

Notes:

Ace of Pentacles

Key - Reward, Riches

Meaning - Pure contentment, attainment, prosperity, bright prospects - both material and spiritual.

Reversed - Unhappiness with wealth, misuse of power, corruption.

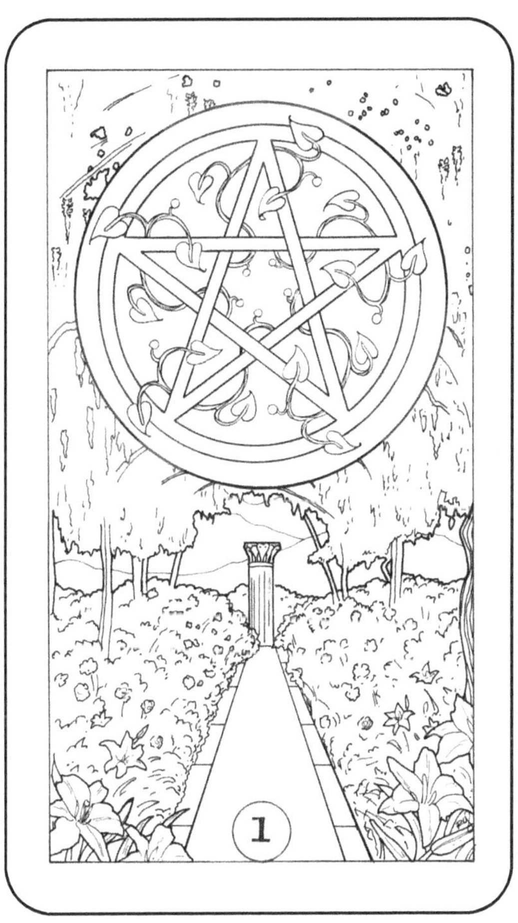

Notes:

King of Pentacles

Key - Riches and Comfort

Meaning - A rich man (materially and spiritually,) steady, reliable, earthy, helpful, sensual.

Reversed - Too materialistic. A tendency toward stupidity and stubbornness. A man who is dangerous when angry. Perverse use of talents. An addiction to physical comfort.

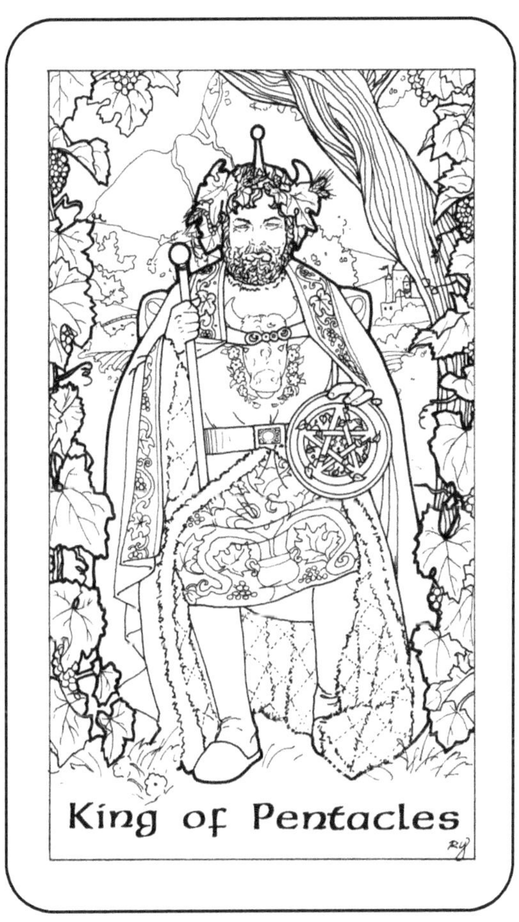

Notes:

Queen of Pentacles

Key - Abundance and Practicality

Meaning - A warm, generous woman - has the Seeker's best interest at heart. Monetary gifts, intelligence, thoughtfulness. No fear of hard work.

Reversed - Too dependent, duties neglected, changeable nature due to fear of failure. Untrusting, false prosperity.

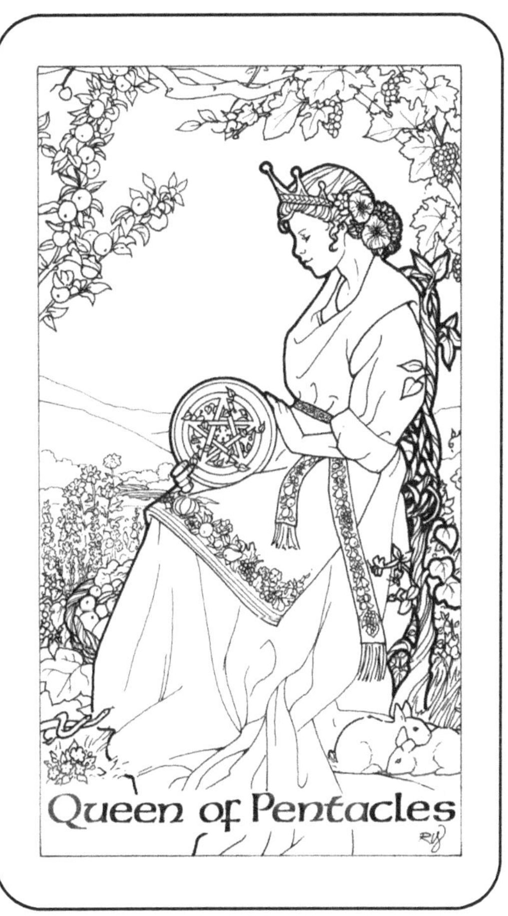

Notes:

Knight of Pentacles

Key - Dependable Help

Meaning - A mature man, responsible, reliable, utilitarian. A person who will help the Seeker. Honorable. Solid. Travel is possible.

Reversed - Problems at work. A warning against travel. The Seeker should guard against deceit, carelessness, inertia, laziness.

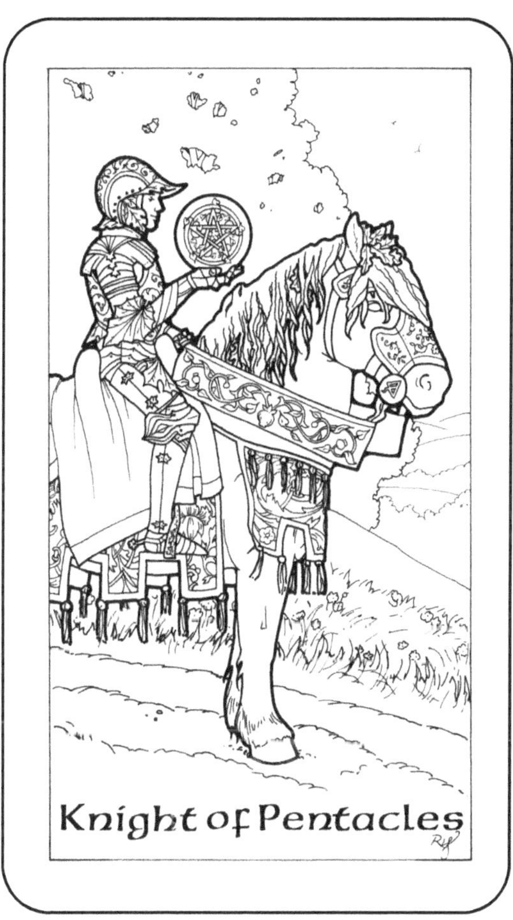

Notes:

Page of Pentacles

Key - Studious Scholarship

Meaning - Deep concentration, scholarship, news, a bringer of messages. A young person makes the seeker proud. A careful child.

Reversed - Bad news, delinquency, illogical thoughts, wastefulness.

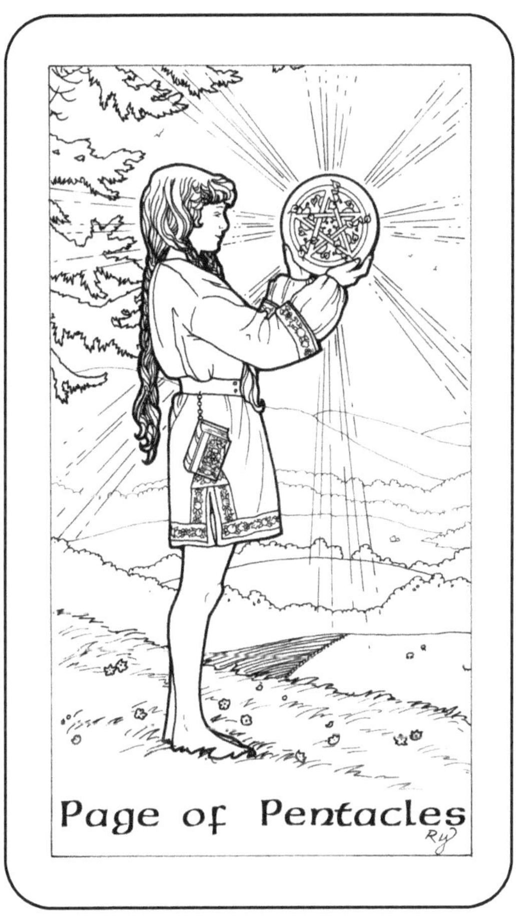

Notes:

Ten of Pentacles

Key - Prosperity

Meaning - Riches. Home, family matters, positive domestic changes.

Reversed - Loss of belongings. An emotional loss or death. Gambling, a bad risk.

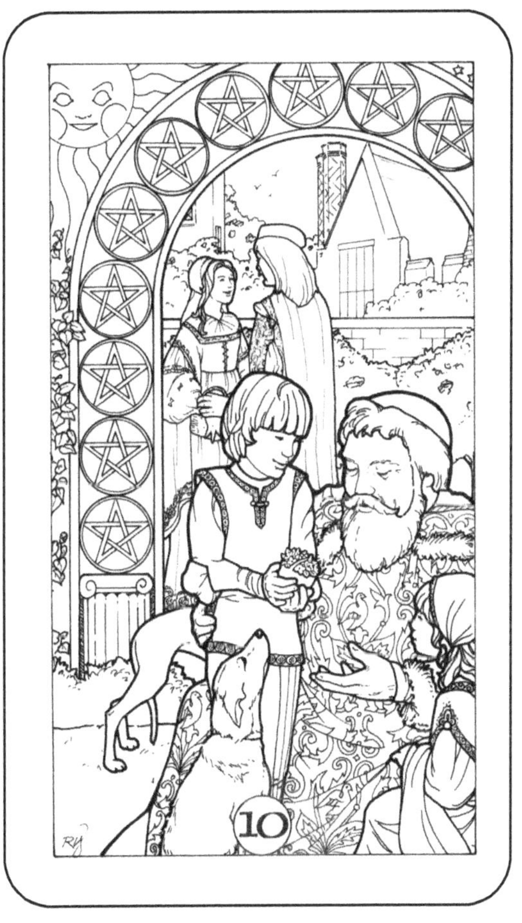

Notes:

Nine of Pentacles

Key - Solitary Wealth and Luxury

Meaning - Accomplishment, discretion, safety, material comfort, love of nature, solitary achievements, working alone, security, femininity.

Reversed - Threat. Loss of security, danger.

PENTACLES

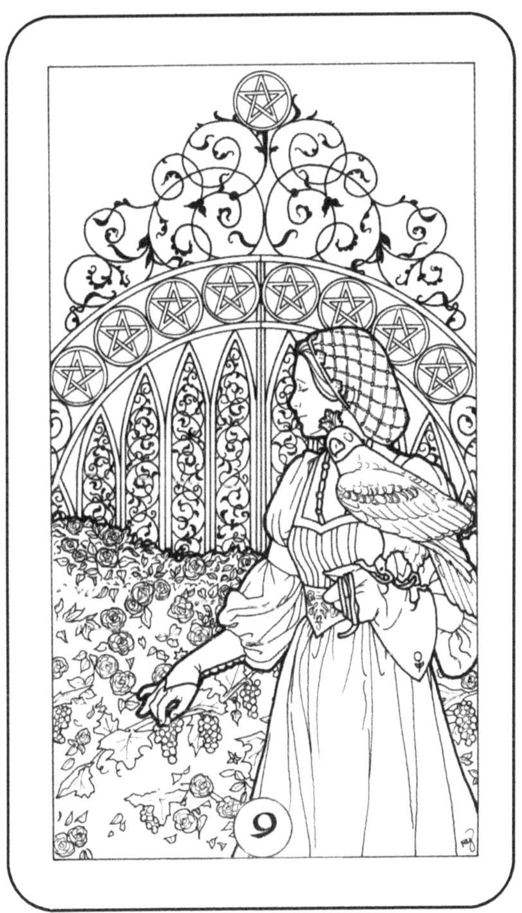

Notes:

Eight of Pentacles

Key - Learning

Meaning - Learning, apprenticeship, internship, gaining new knowledge or skills, working very hard at low-paying levels, nose to the grindstone. Creation.

Reversed - A lack of emotion, vanity. Caution against borrowing money.

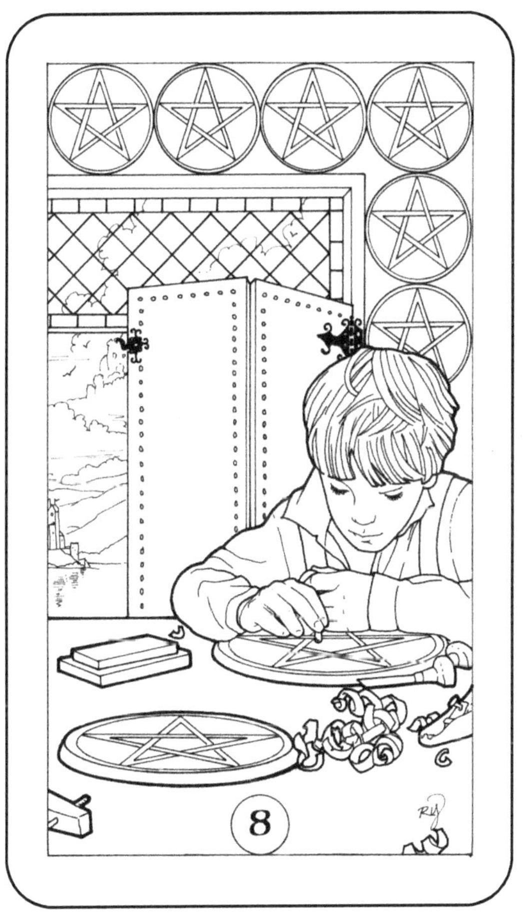

Notes:

Seven of Pentacles

Key - Material progress

Meaning - Cleverness, growth through hard work. Surprisingly good news. Help will prove useful.

Reversed - Money lost. Bad investments. Anxiety about finances.

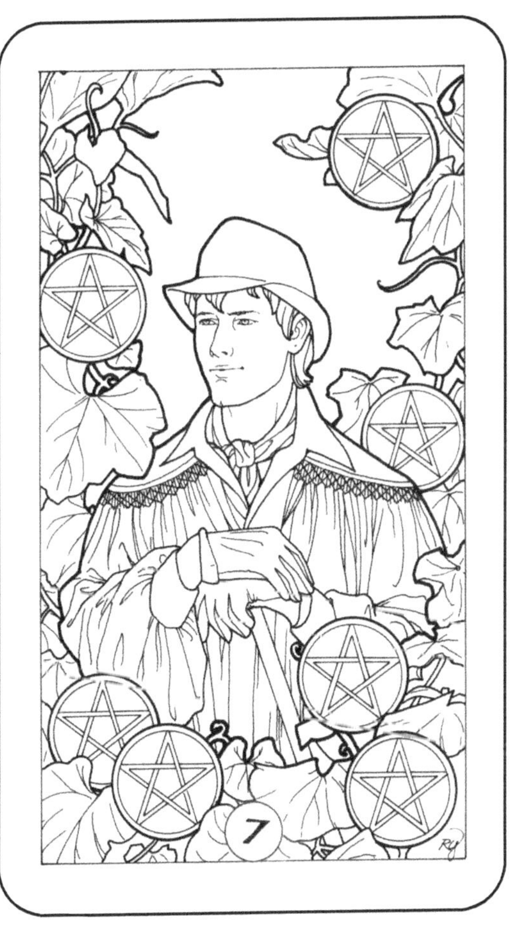

Notes:

Six of Pentacles

Key - Gratification

Meaning - Help with finances. Return of a favor. Gifts, stability. Gratifying your desire to help or repay another.

Reversed - Jealousy can cause harm. Unstable finances frustrate plans. Desire, avarice. A bad debt.

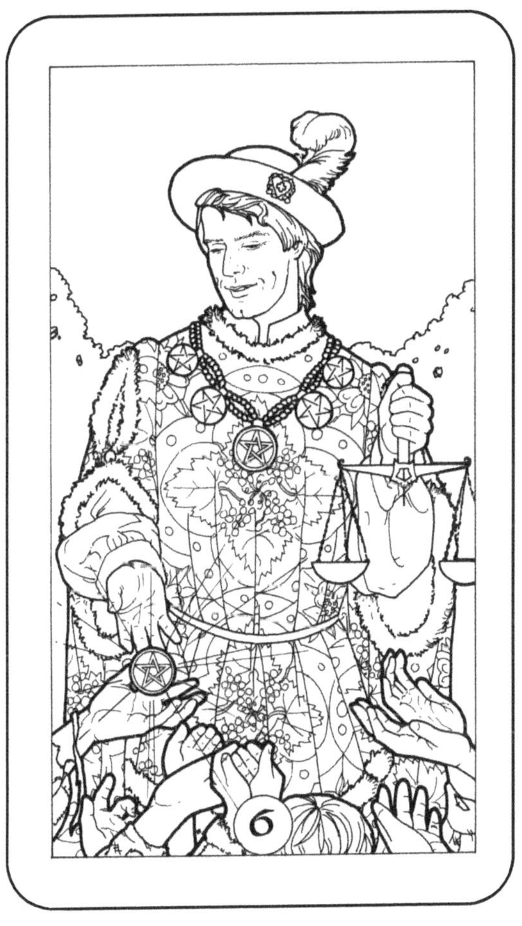

Notes:

Five of Pentacles

Key - Misery

Meaning - Destitution, los, loneliness, being out in the cold. Lovers who cannot find a meeting place. Poor health, spiritual impoverishment.

Reversed - Lessons in charity to be learned. New employment (possibly temporary.) New courage. new interest in spiritual matters.

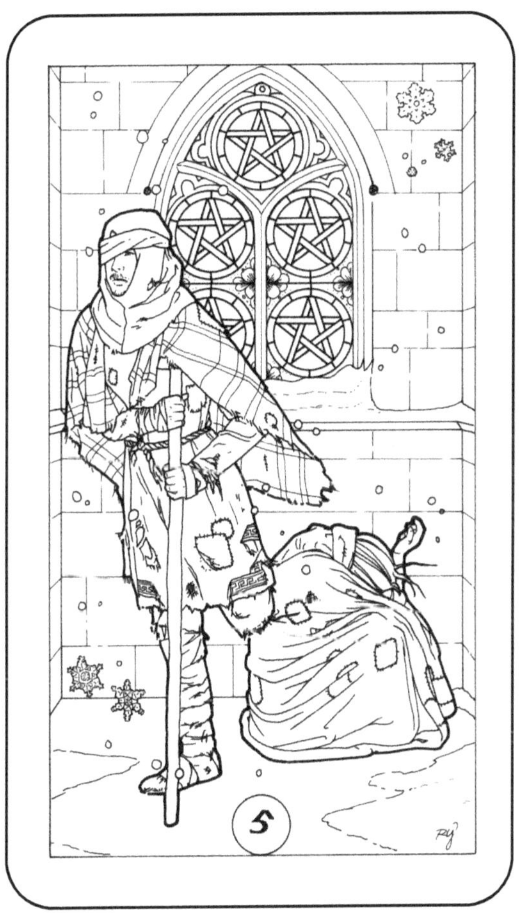

Notes:

Four of Pentacles

Key - Miser

Meaning - miserliness, greed, selfishness. Avarice, suspicion, mistrust. Inability to let go of anything. An emotional black hole. Shortsightedness, imbalance, desperation.

Reversed - Suspense of gain, opposition, reversal of fortune.

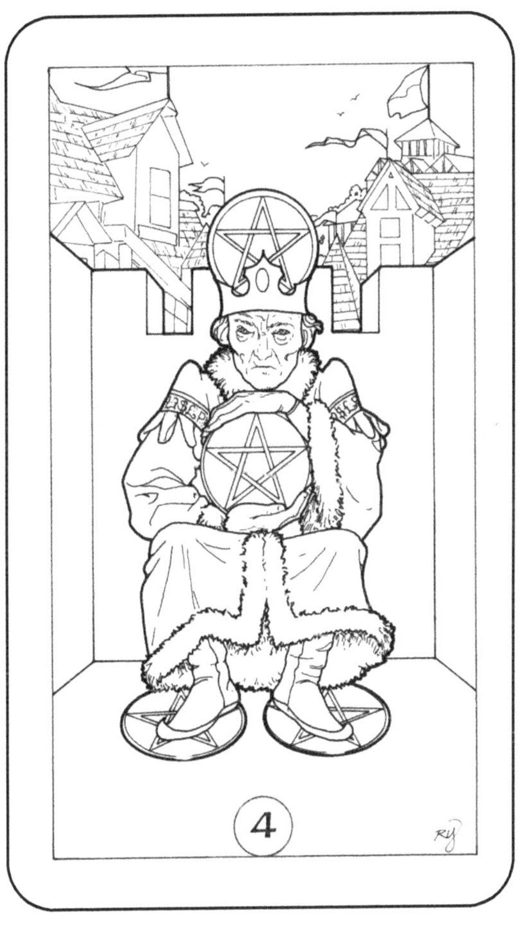

Notes:

Three of Pentacles

Key - Master craftsman

Meaning - Skills and abilities will be appreciated and rewarded. Success through effort. Artistic ability, rank, power, achievement.

Reversed - Sloppy workmanship. Delay of recognition or recompense. Preoccupation with gain at the cost of craft. Mediocrity.

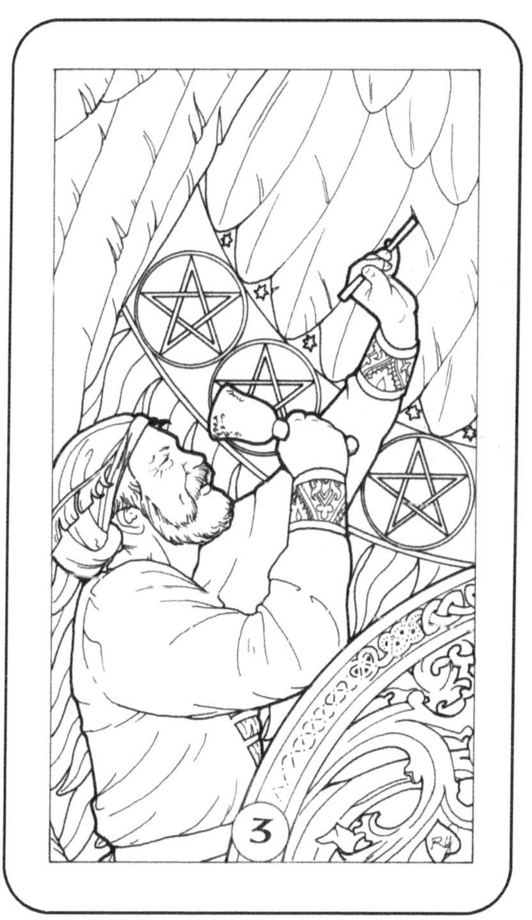

Notes:

Two of Pentacles

Key - The Juggler, balance

Meaning - Ability to handle several things at once. Harmony in the midst of conflict and change. Fun and games. Knowing the ropes. Balance in self and in life. Control.

Reversed - Too much to handle. Instability. Lack of control. Forced gaiety.

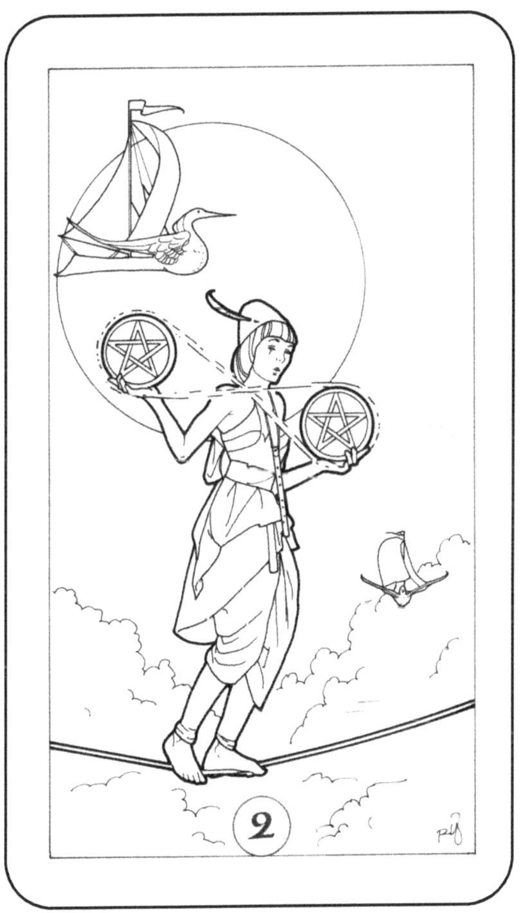

Notes:

Ace of Swords

Key - Knowledge Victorious

Meaning - The Seeker might be a champion, a hero, or a leader. The birth of a valiant child may be indicated. Attainment of power or goals.

Reversed - Destruction. Obstacles. Tyranny. Excessive use of force. A separation. Beware of using too much power to gain your ends.

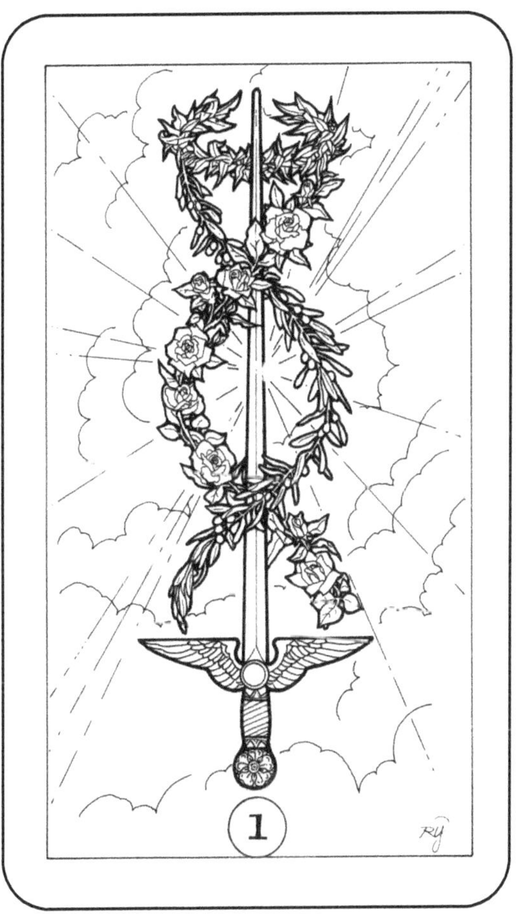

Notes:

King of Swords

Key - The Boss

Meaning - A perceptive, strong-willed, intelligent man.

Reversed - Cruel and hardhearted. Untrustworthy, crafty, pig-headed.

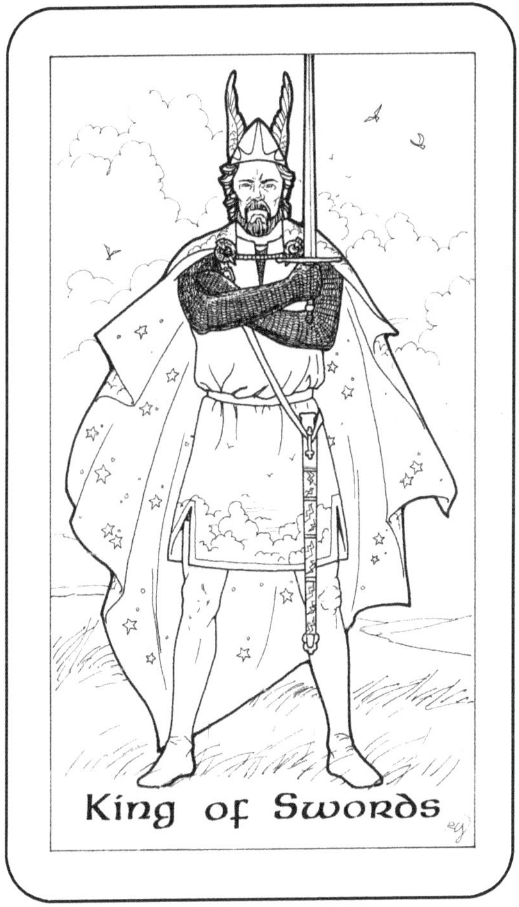

Notes:

Queen of Swords

Key - Cool and Confident

Meaning - A strong woman, intensely perceptive, confident, and quick-witted.

Reversed - Keenness sharpened to cruelty. Sly, deceitful, narrow minded, quarrelsome. A gossip.

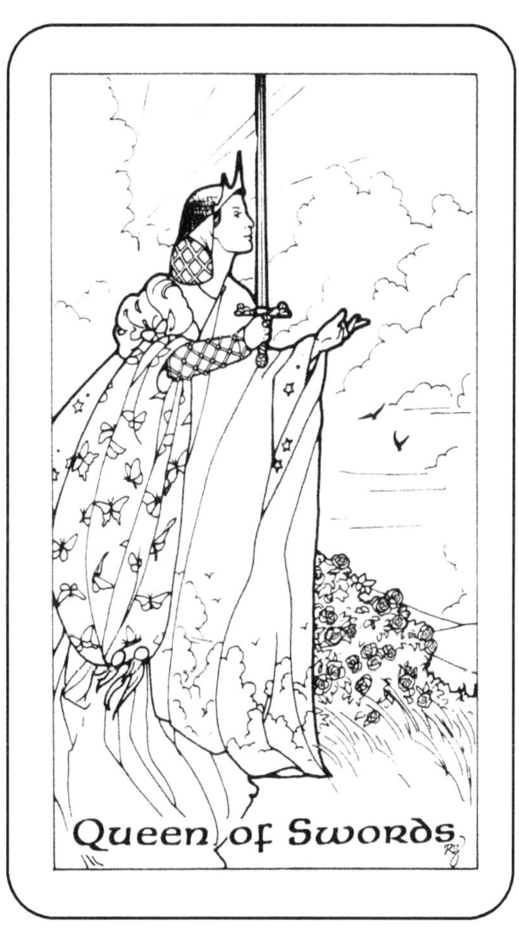

SWORDS

Notes:

Knight of Swords

Key - To Boldly Go

Meaning - A soldier; heroic, brave. Righteous anger. Triumph over opposition. A practical solution to a problem.

Reversed - Unsuccessful or erratic behavior. Bad judgement, extravagance. The seeker makes an impulsive mistake.

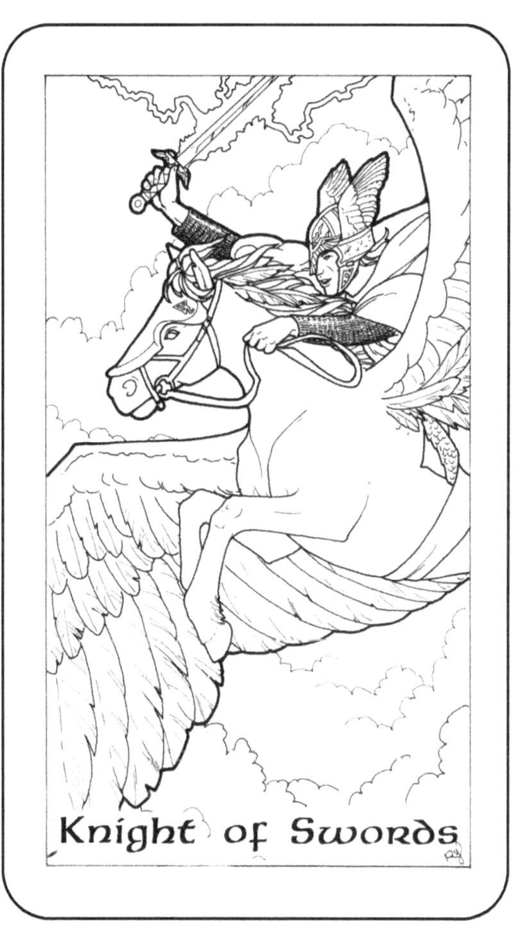

Notes:

Page of Swords

Key - Running with Scissors

Meaning - Vigilance, agility, insight, keenness of vision. Service done in secret. The Seeker obtains the help of a younger person.

Reversed - Childish cruelty. Unfortunate circumstances. The unforeseen. Vulnerability in the face of opposing force.

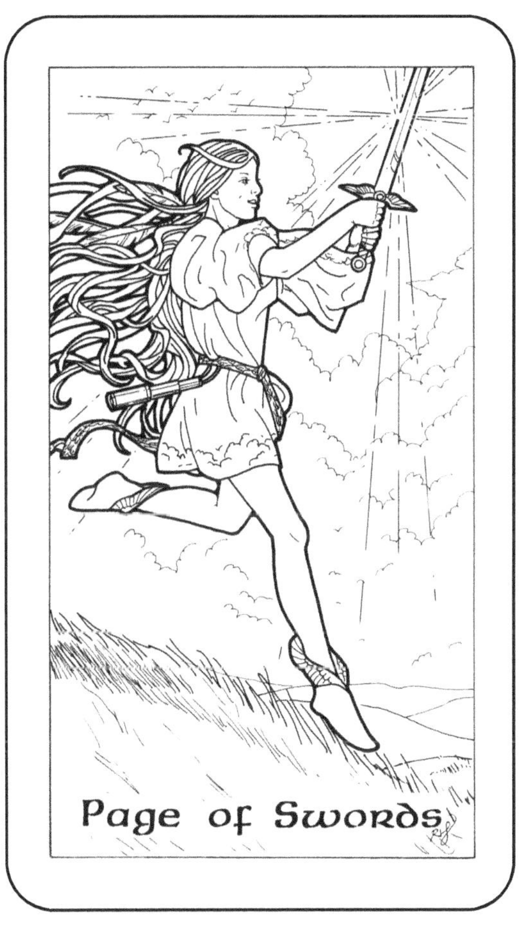

SWORDS

Notes:

Ten of Swords

Key - No, It Really IS That Bad!

Meaning - Misfortune, ruin, defeat, loss, failure, pain, desolation beyond tears. Alternatively, evils or misfortunes which are over.

Reversed - Evil overthrown, courage, success, recovery, turning toward higher sources.

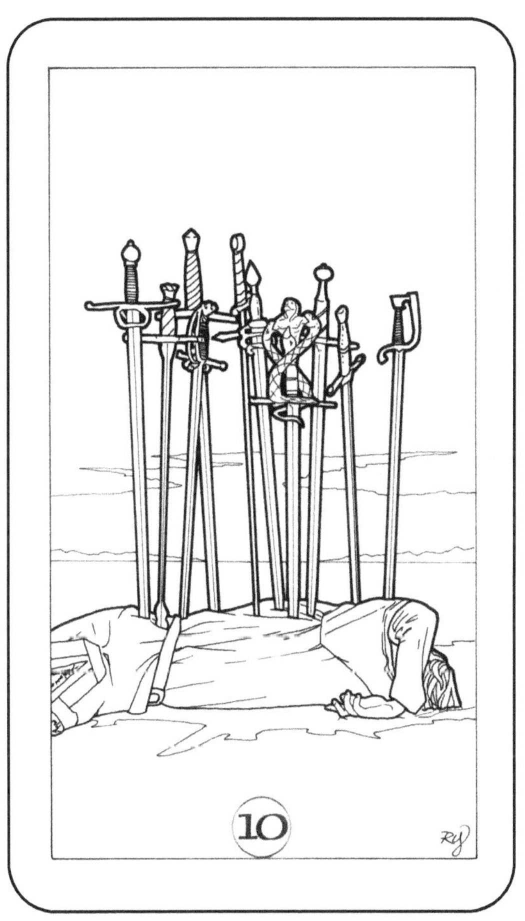

Notes:

Nine of Swords

Key - Night Terrors

Meaning - Suffering, desolation, doubt, suspicion, misery, dishonesty, slander, a vicious circle. Illness or injury to a loved one. Alternatively troubles which aren't over yet. The worst is yet to come.

Reversed - End of suffering, desolation, doubt. Good news about a loved one. Patience, faithfulness.

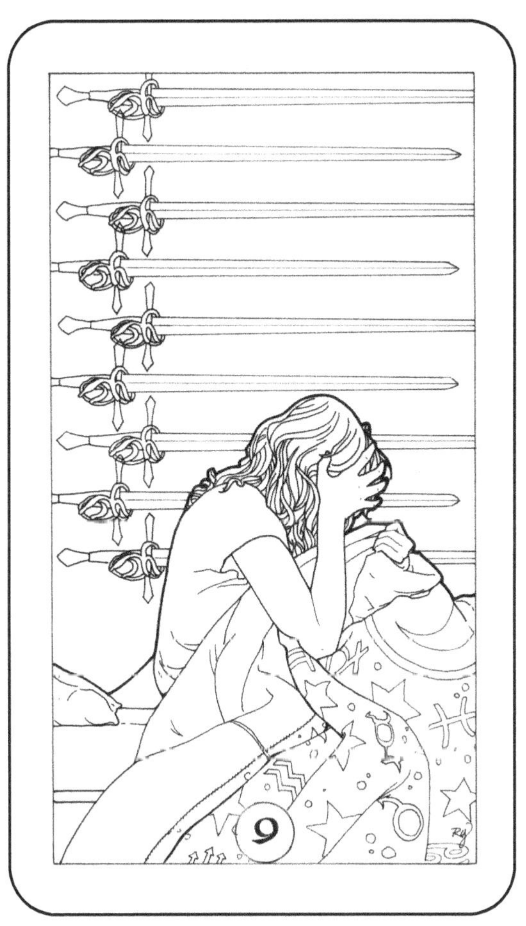

Notes:

Eight of Swords

Key - I Just Can't!

Meaning - Fear, bondage, paralysis due to indecision, censure, illness, difficulties. Can symbolize prison. A nearly impossible task.

Reversed - Respite from fear, new beginnings, freedom, release.

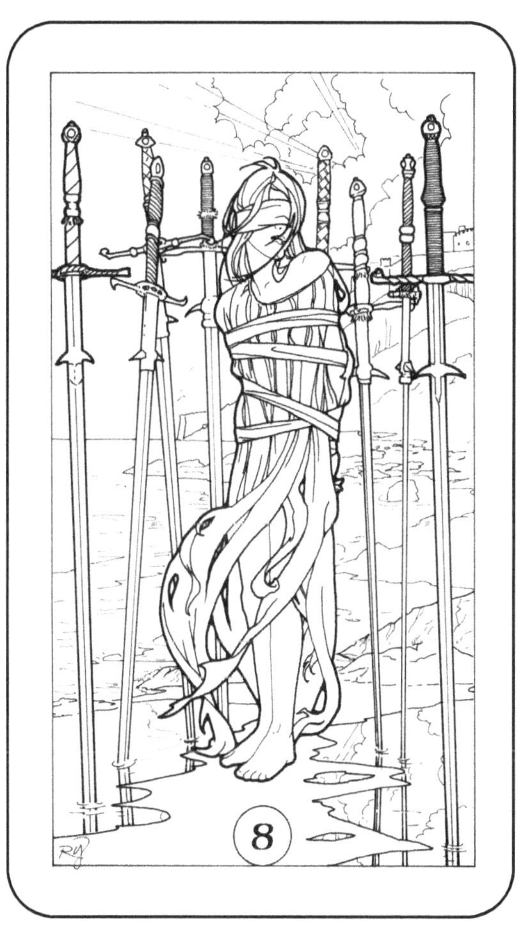

Notes:

Seven of Swords

Key - Thief

Meaning - Taking something with belongs to another, unreliability, betrayal, spying. Failure of a plan. A less-than-honorable action. Or, depending on surrounding cards, bravery and care. Stealth.

Reversed - Over-qualification, good advice, return of stolen property.

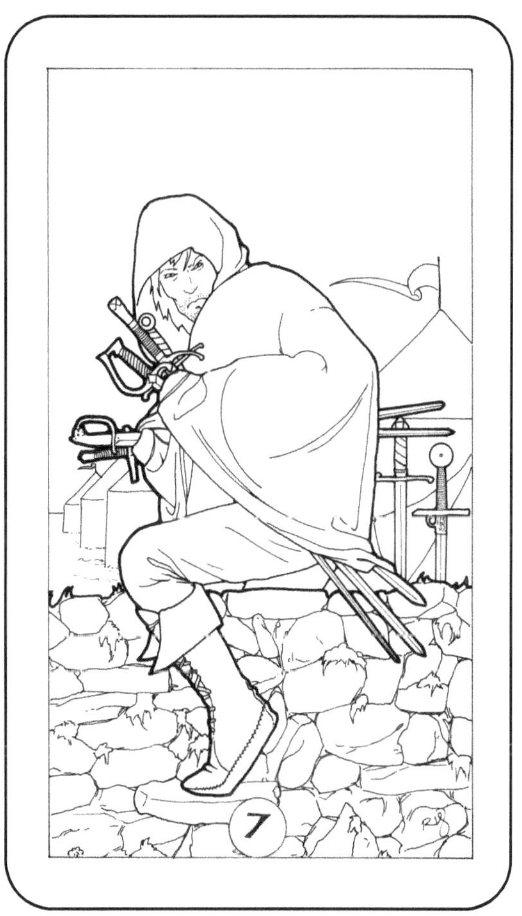

Notes:

Six of Swords

Key - Rite of Passage

Meaning - Passage to a higher state of consciousness. Leaving difficulties for a safe refuge. A water journey. Finding understanding.

Reversed - No escape. Journey postponed. A trip to a higher level of consciousness is advised.

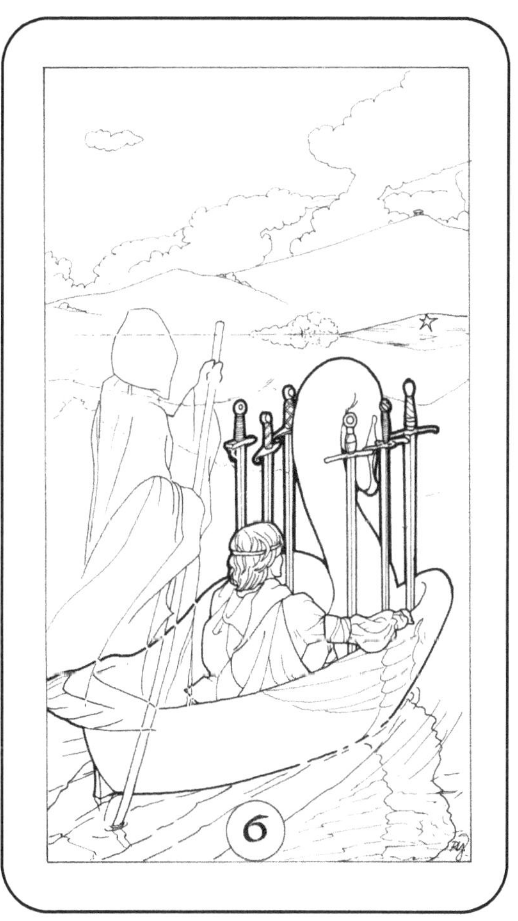

Notes:

Five of Swords

Key - Nyaa-nya-nya-nyaa-nya

Meaning - Failure, defeat, degradation, winning by unfair means, trickery, cowardice, manipulation. A loss decreed by the gods.

Reversed - Same as upright meaning, but lessened. An empty victory. Unfairness and slyness in dealing with others.

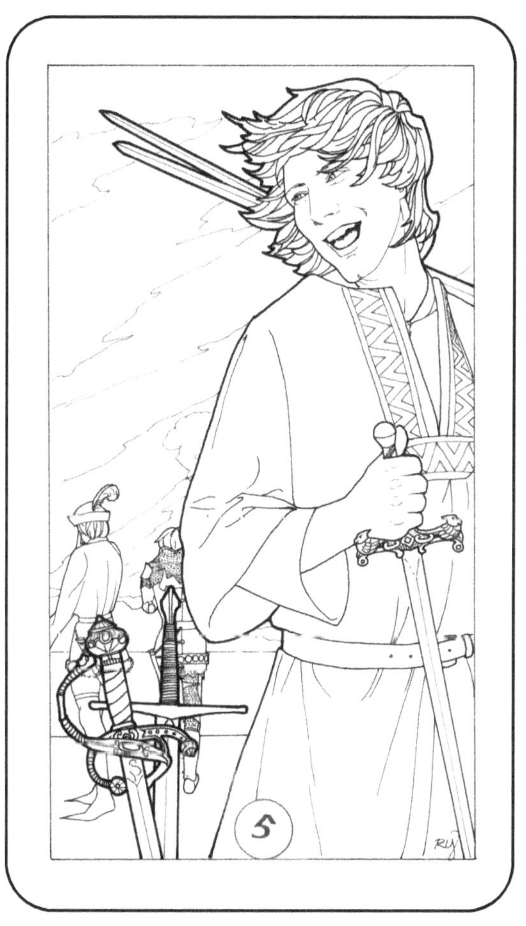

Notes:

Four of Swords

Key - Restful Private Place

Meaning - Rest, seclusion, convalescence. A return to the basics. Meditation.

Reversed - An end to rest. A return to active life.

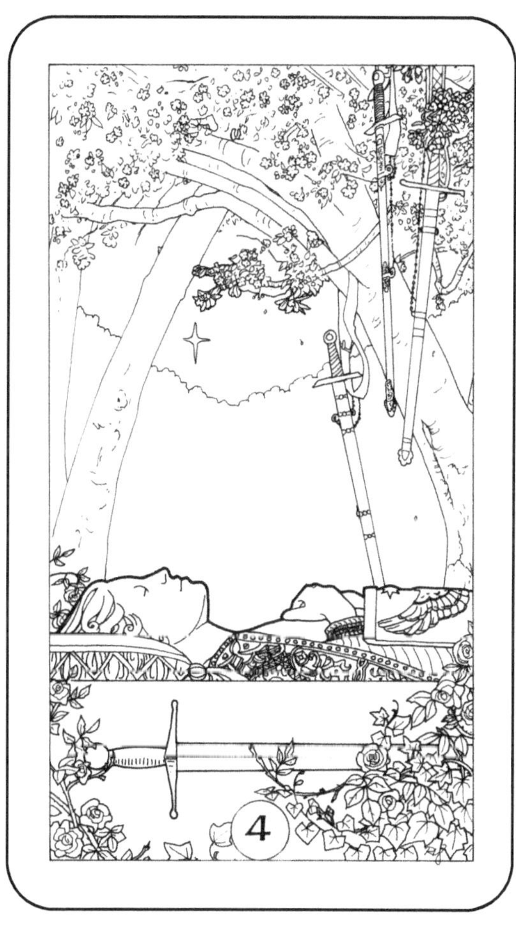

Notes:

Three of Swords

Key - Tears and Woe

Meaning - Sorrow, loss, emotional pain, separation, grief. The end of an affair of the heart.

Reversed - Same as upright meaning, but not as extreme.

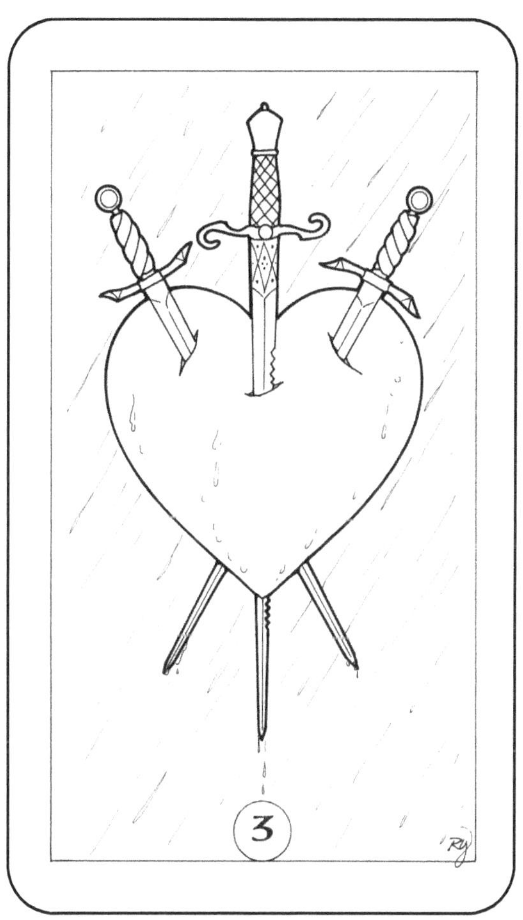

Notes:

Two of Swords

Key - Balance

Meaning - Dangerous spot, precarious balance. Possible problems ahead. A choice of the lesser of two evils. The Seeker has the knowledge and ability to balance the situation and make the best of it.

Reversed - The waiting is over. Stalement ended. Beware of a new situation. The Seeker, or someone they know, may travel soon.

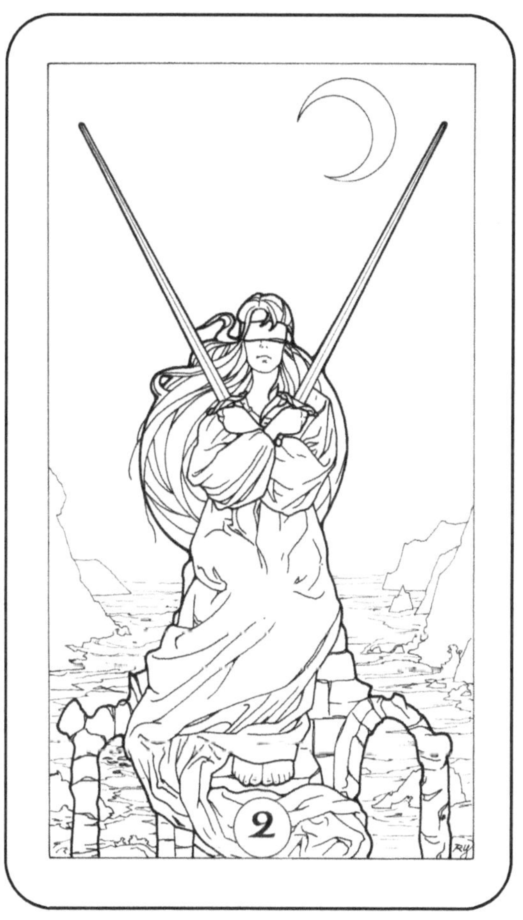

Notes:

Ace of Wands

Key - Creation and Power, New Life

Meaning - Beginning, life, growth, energy, virility, fertility, inheritance, birth, adventure.

Reversed - False start, unrealized goal, decadence, stagnation, sterility.

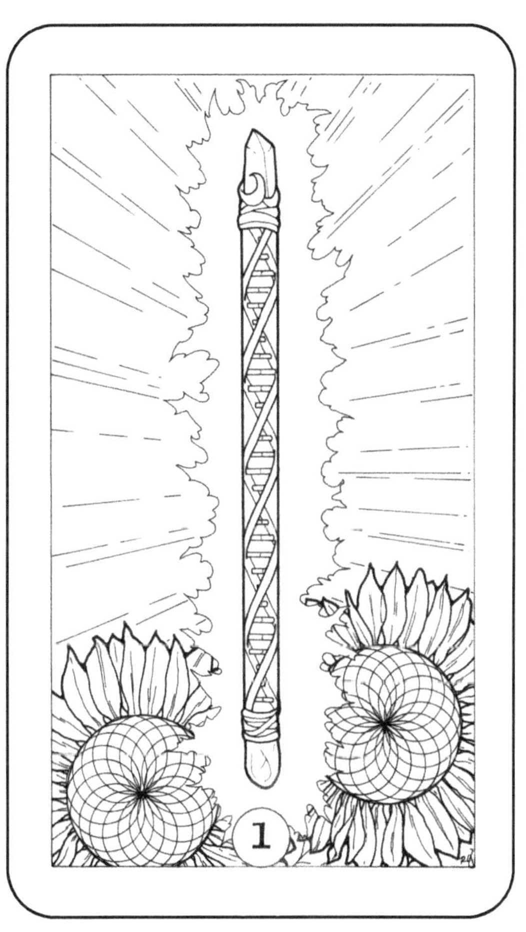

Notes:

King of Wands

Key - I Am

Meaning - A man of passion, handsome, conscientious, noble, strong. Sometimes hasty.

Reversed - A severe man, harsh, opinionated, strict, quarrelsome. Sometimes intolerant or prejudiced.

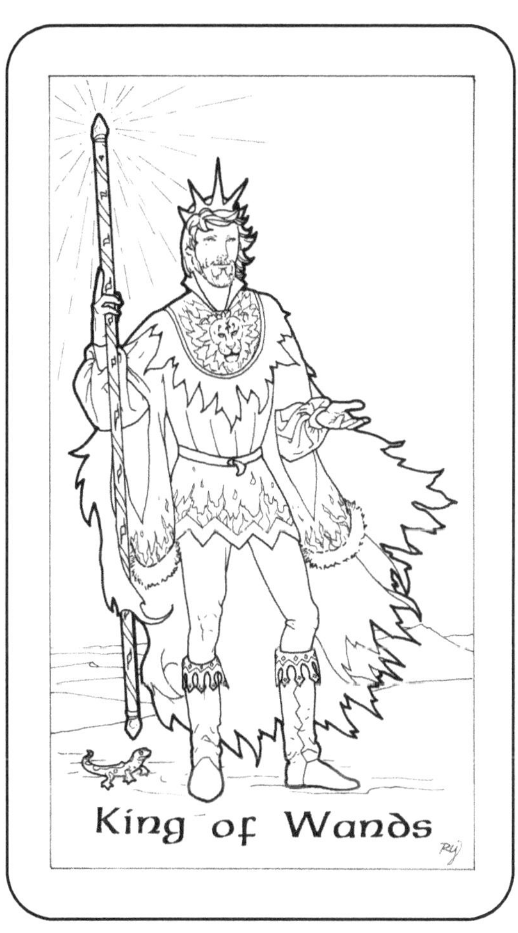

Notes:

Queen of Wands

Key - Welcome

Meaning - A woman of considerable energy, very active, very passionate. Fond of nature, generous, and practical.

Reversed - Strict, domineering, jealous, vengeful. A deceitful woman. Passion overrules all other concerns. A tendency towards unfaithfulness.

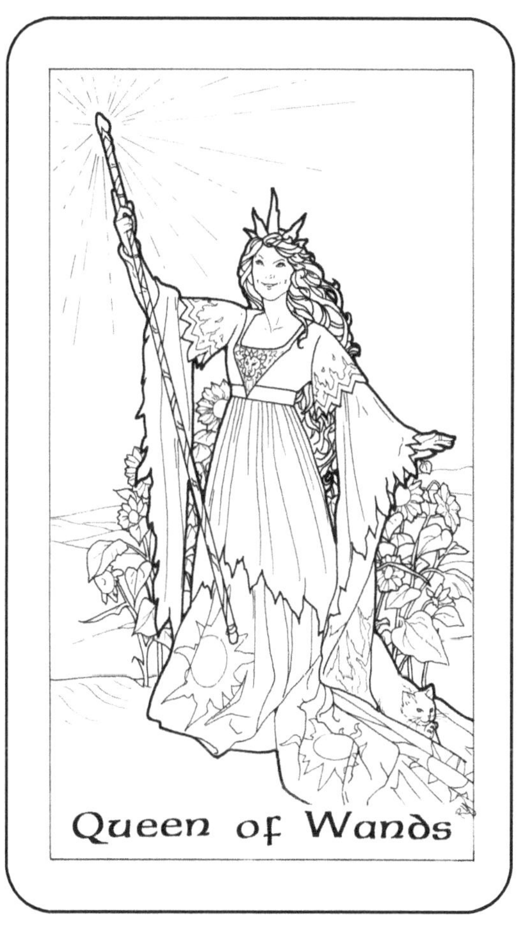

Notes:

Knight of Wands

Key - Where Angels Fear to Tread

Meaning - A journey. Practical action taken in spite of distractions. A change of residence.

Reversed - Separation, discord, misunderstanding, progress interrupted. A quarrel.

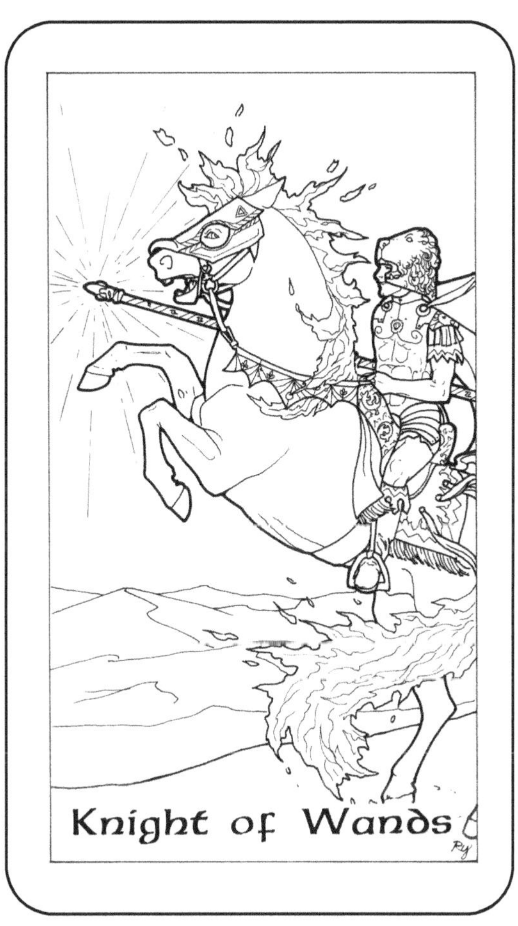

Notes:

Page of Wands

Key - Hearken!

Meaning - A child with too much energy. A faithful of loyal person. A stranger explodes into the Seeker's life with good intentions. A great idea leading to success. A good employee.

Reversed - Childish pranks, bad news, indecision. The behavior of an acquaintance leads the Seeker to doubt his or her sincerity. A gossip.

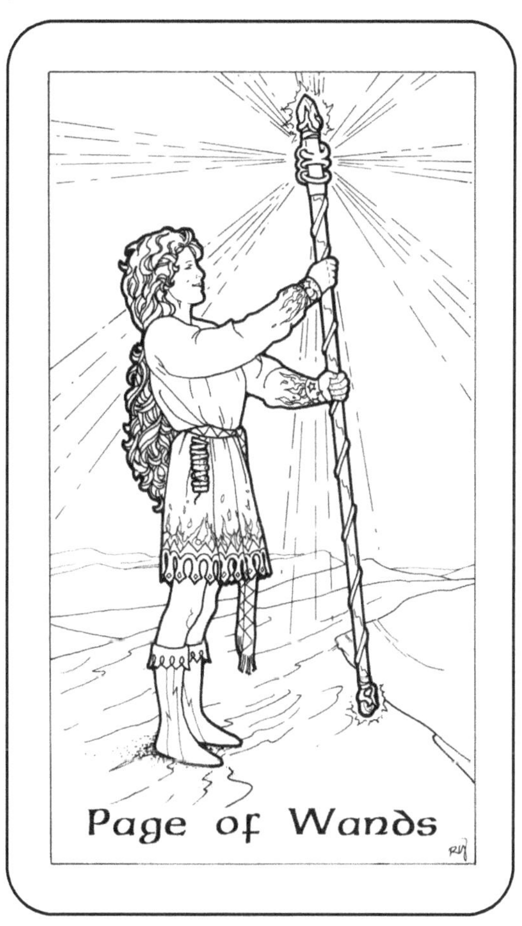

Notes:

Ten of Wands

Key - Overload

Meaning - Too much success becomes oppressive. Heavy burden. Martyr complex. Too much willingness to carry others' responsibilities. Taking on more than the Seeker can handle.

Reversed - Selfishness, shifting responsibility to another. Passing the buck.

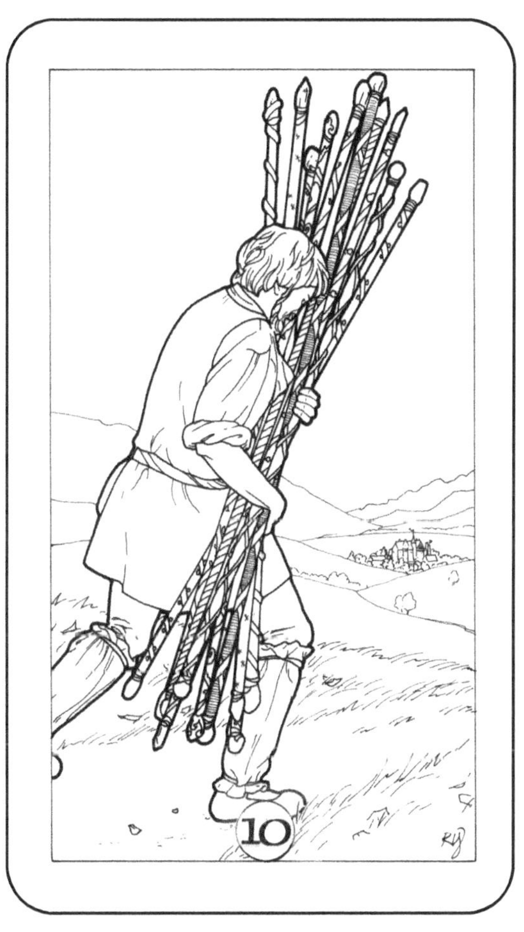

Notes:

Nine of Wands

Key - Wait For It

Meaning - Waiting for difficulties, changes, new challenges. Hidden foes, deception. Temporary cease-fire in struggles.

Reversed - Obstacles, problems, calamity, illness, disability.

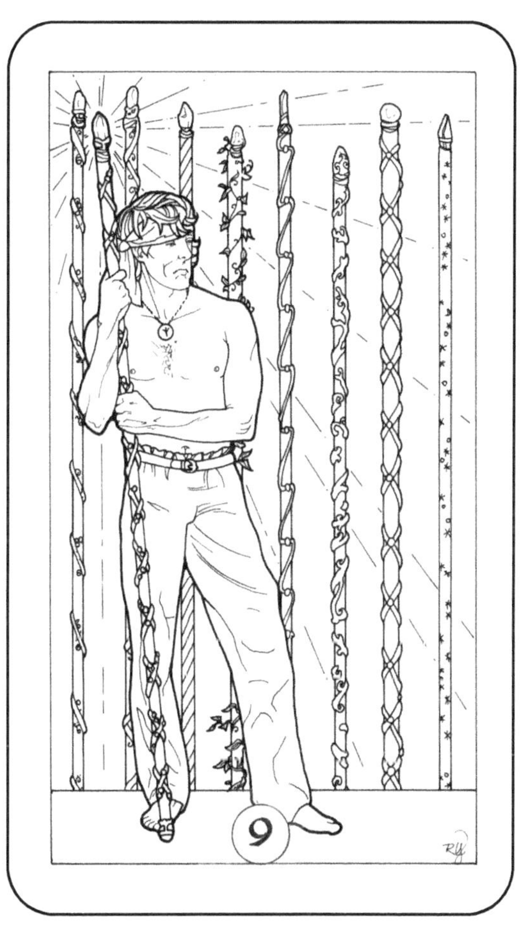

Notes:

Eight of Wands

Key - Sudden Advancement

Meaning - Swift activity, the path of activity, hope. Freedom of action after a period of inaction. Too swift a pace. Decisions made in haste. Travel.

Reversed - Jealousy, dispute, oppressive conditions at home or work. A bad conscience.

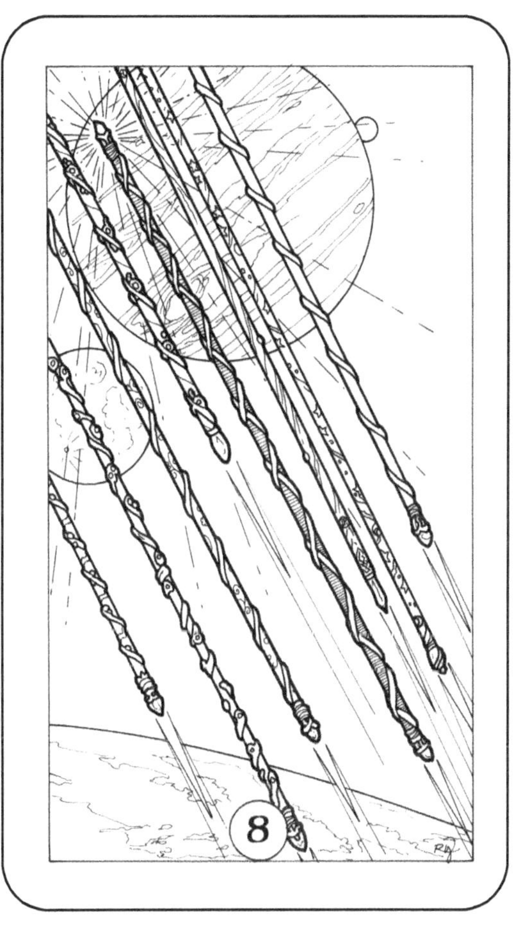

Notes:

Seven of Wands

Key - Take a Stand

Meaning - Success agains obstacles, problems solved or turned aside. Bravery.

Reversed - Misgivings about an outcome, perplexity, anxiety. Hesitancy causes a loss.

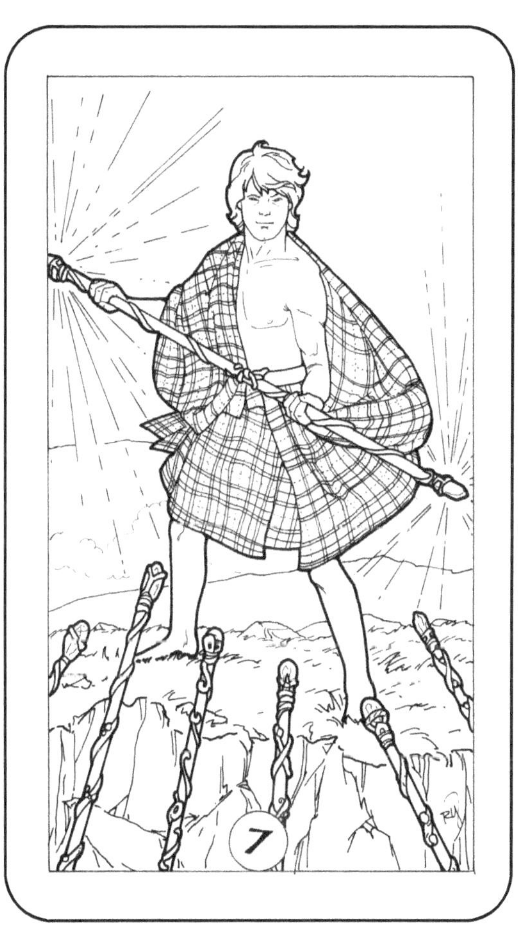

Notes:

Six of Wands

Key - Triumph

Meaning - Public acclamation, good or important news, gain, achievement, reward for hard work, great expectations.

Reversed - Delay, fear, disloyalty, inconclusive victory, acclaim with no real substance.

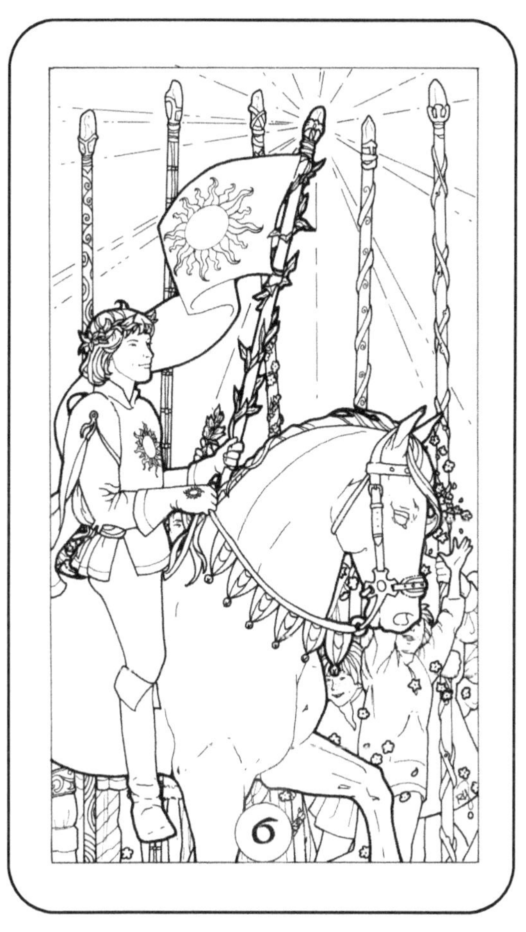

Notes:

Five of Wands

Key - Unfulfilled Struggle

Meaning - Conflict, obstacles, unsatisfied desires, internal strife, indecision.

Reversed - Trickery, complexity, involvement.

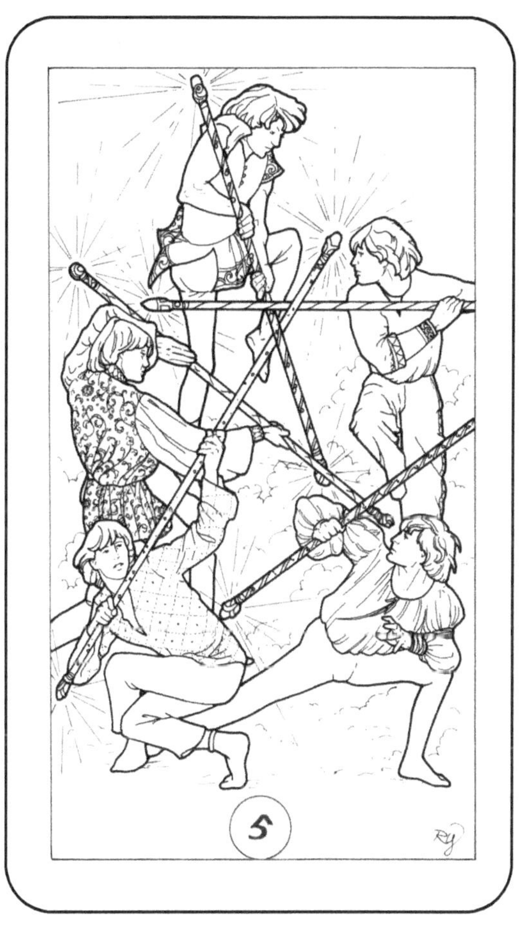

Notes:

Four of Wands

Key - Romance and Tranquility

Meaning - Harmony, romance, a wedding. Society, newly acquired prosperity, fruits of labor, rest, harvest, home.

Reversed - Loss of tranquility, ingratitude, dissatisfaction with present situation.

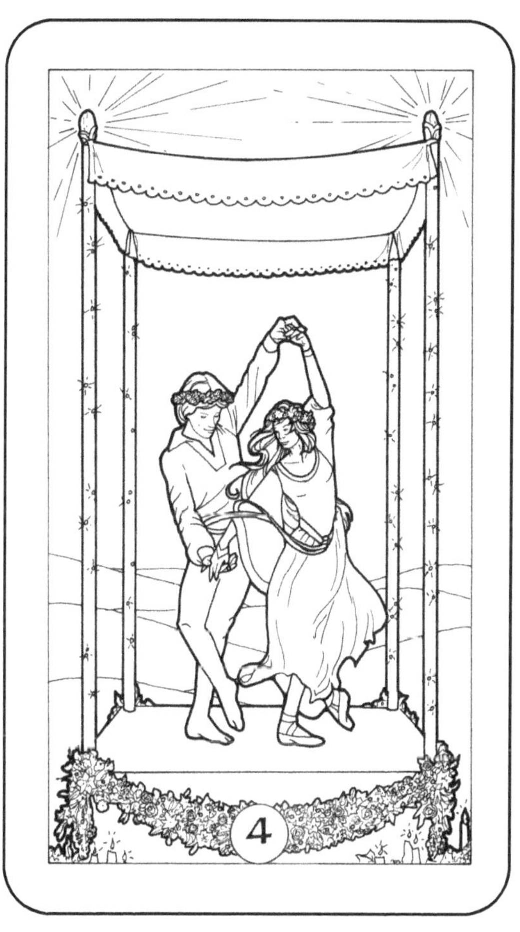

Notes:

Three of Wands

Key - Ships Coming In

Meaning - Good business, strength, grasp of future and of things needed for growth, successful business ventures.

Reversed - Bad business, failed business ventures, poor grasp of the future.

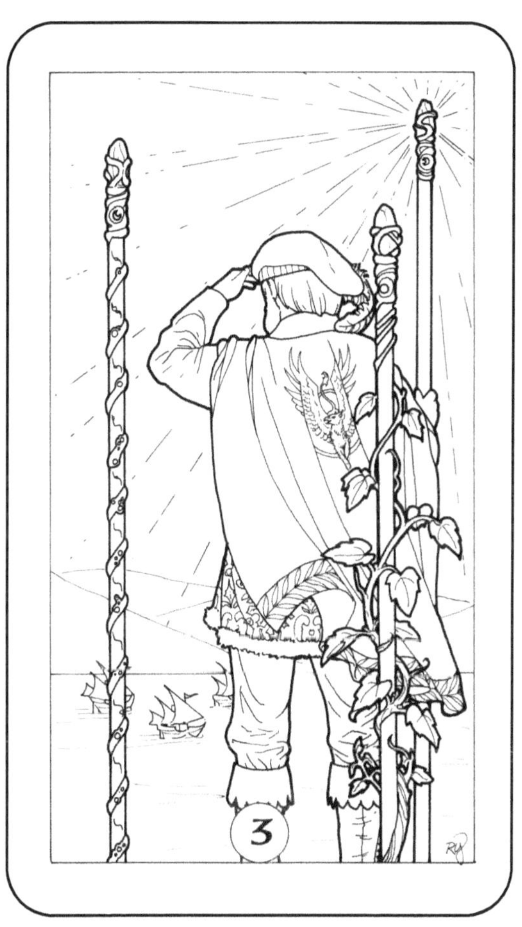

Notes:

Two of Wands

Key - Watch and Wait

Meaning - Wait to see if plans bear fruit. Kindness, generosity, intellect, well-balanced individual, creative. Good things coming, fulfillment.

Reversed - Seeker must avoid impatience. Empty success. Good beginnings go sour. Domination by others.

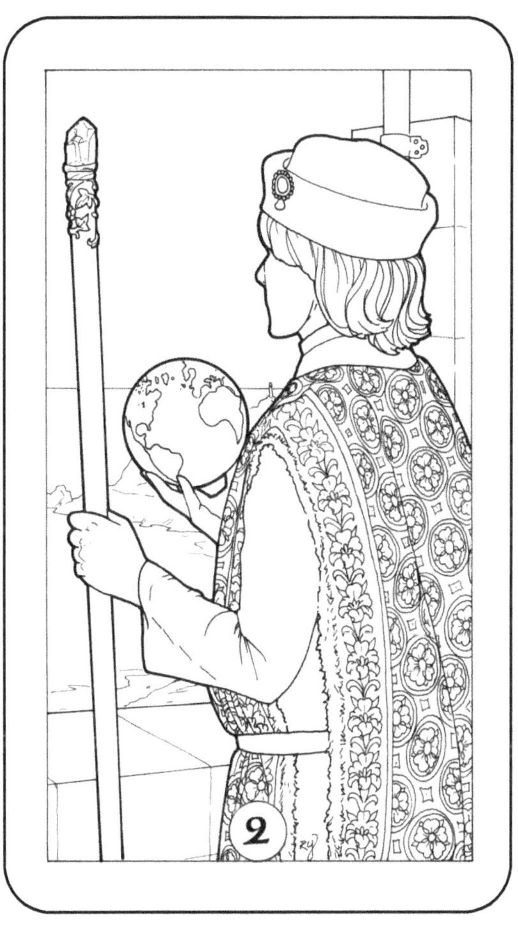

Notes:

Ace of Cups

Key - Bounty

Meaning - Joy, abundance, perfection, fulfillment, fertility, good things overflowing, fullness. Favorable outlook, faithfulness. Love.

Reversed - False hope, clouded joy, fulfillment delayed, false heart, unfaithfulness, false love, change, alteration, sterility.

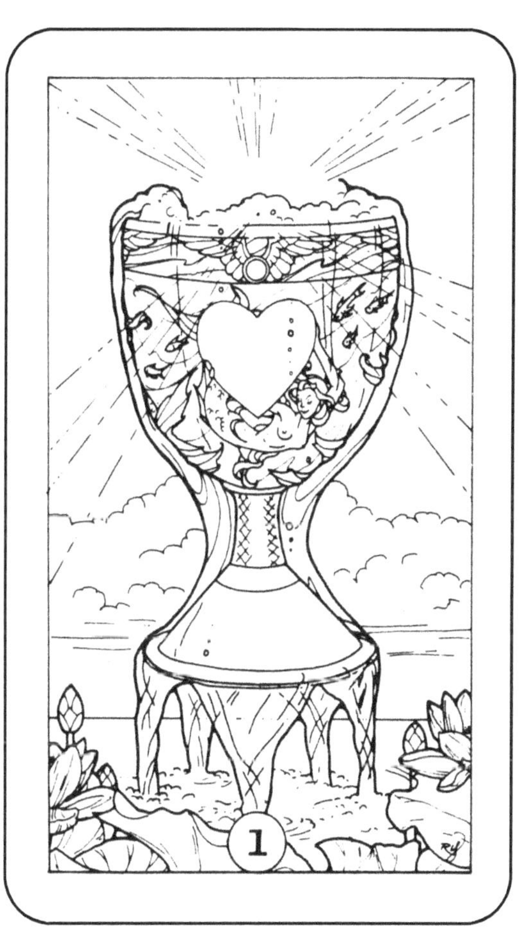

Notes:

King of Cups

Key - Gentle Father

Meaning - A kind, considerate man, a father figure, interested in the arts, balanced. A deep man with a quiet demeanor. Quiet power.

Reversed - A powerful, two-faced man. A violent man. A double-crosser.

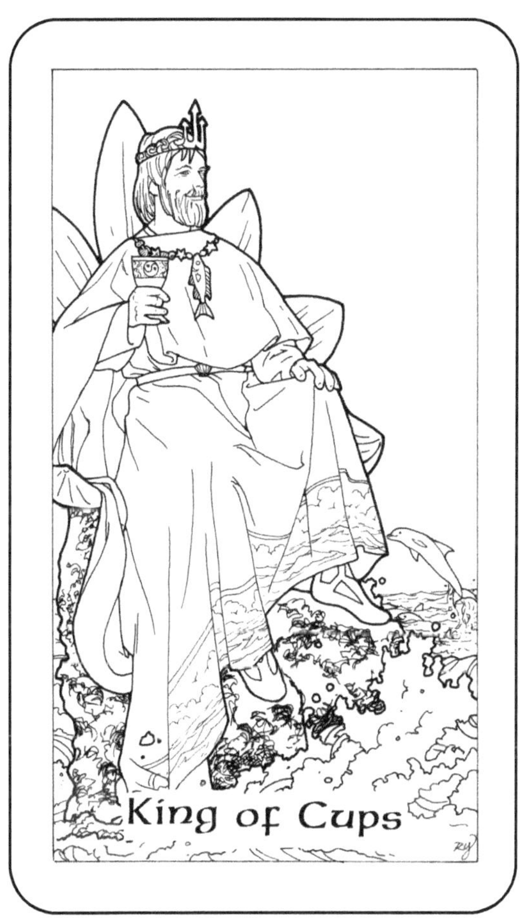

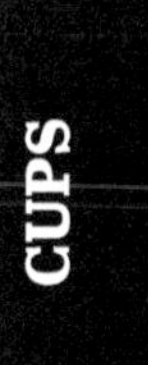

Notes:

Queen of Cups

Key - Loving Mother

Meaning - A soft, nurturing mother figure, perhaps too protective. Kind but not energetic. Will help if it's not too taxing. Good insight, love, gentleness.

Reversed - Too much imagination. Too passive. An overprotective mother who "means well" or is "only thinking of you, dear." A woman who stifles her children.

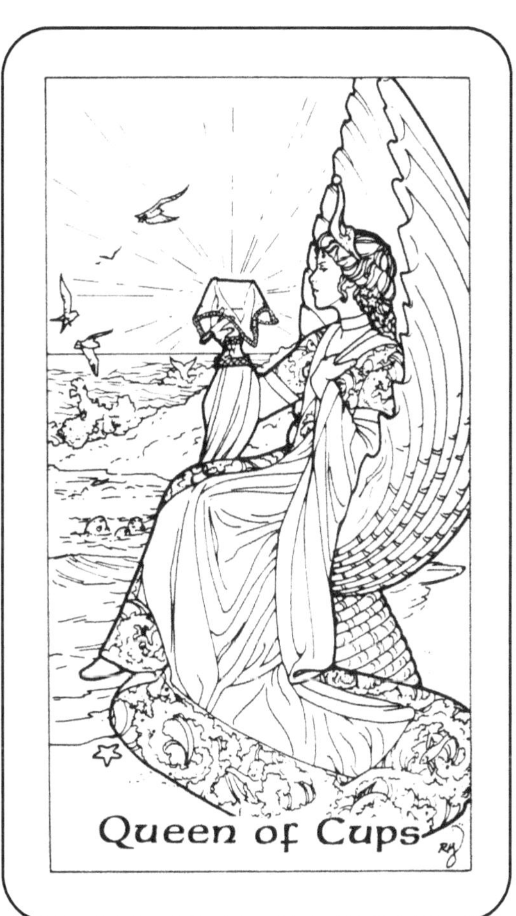

Notes:

Knight of Cups

Key - The Lover Arrives

Meaning - An opportunity may be presented to the Seeker. The arrival of a lover. Approach, appeal, creativity, inspiration. Someone who wears their heart on their sleeve.

Reversed - A person capable of trickery. Warning against fraud. Competition for a love.

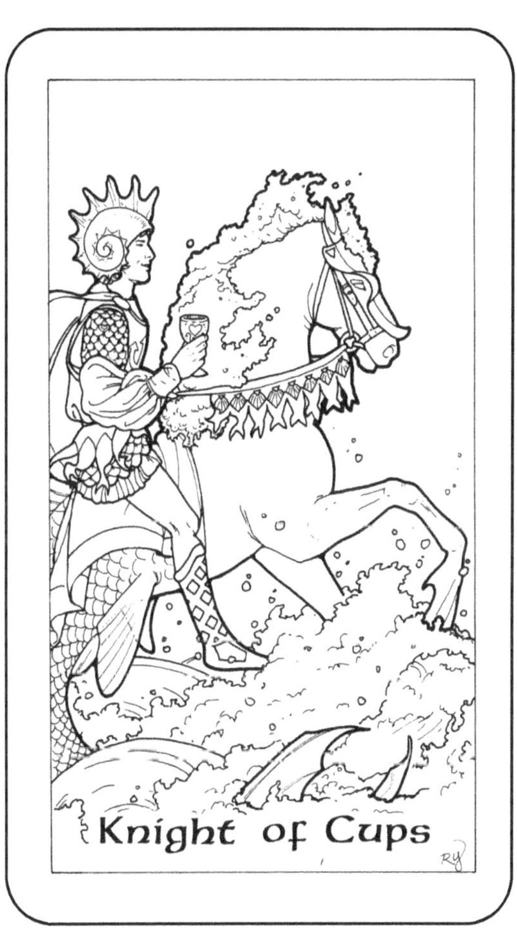

Notes:

Page of Cups

Key - Developing Talent

Meaning - A helpful youth of artistic temperament, studious an intense. A trustworthy and trusting employee. The seeker finds that a child brings joy. A birth.

Reversed - Deception, poor taste, seduction, inclination. A lack of discretion. An unpleasant surprise.

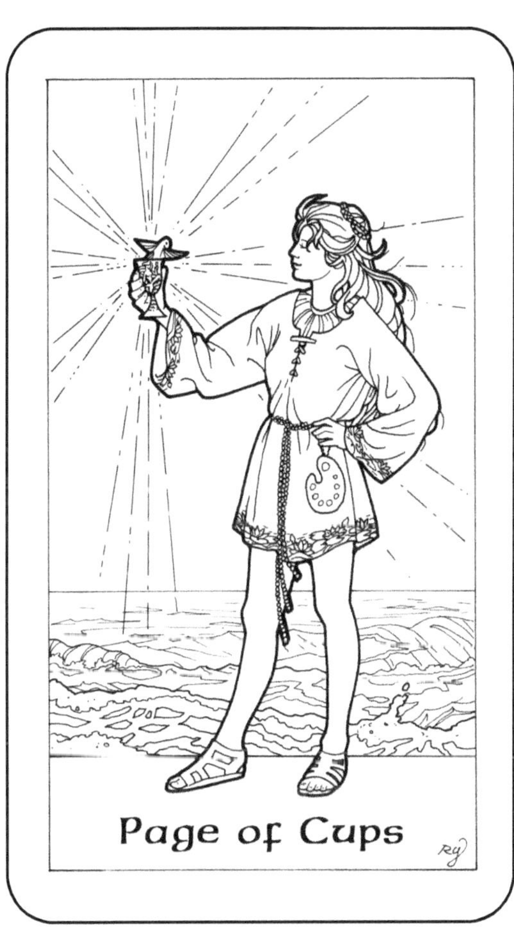

Notes:

Ten of Cups

Key - Welcome Home

Meaning - Home, joy, familial bliss. Peace. Plenty. Love. Contentment of the heart. Respect from your neighbors.

Reversed - The loss of a friendship. Sadness or great disappointment. Indignation.

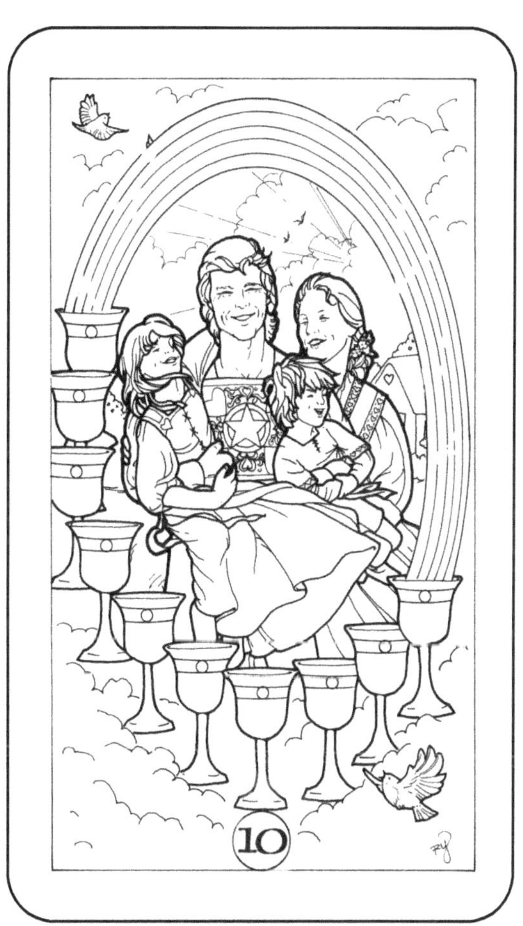

Notes:

Nine of Cups

Key - Party Hearty

Meaning - Satisfaction, plenty, well-being, success, security, sensual pleasures, wishes fulfilled.

Reversed - An absence of upright qualities. Self-indulgent behavior, smugness, deprivation or temporary illness.

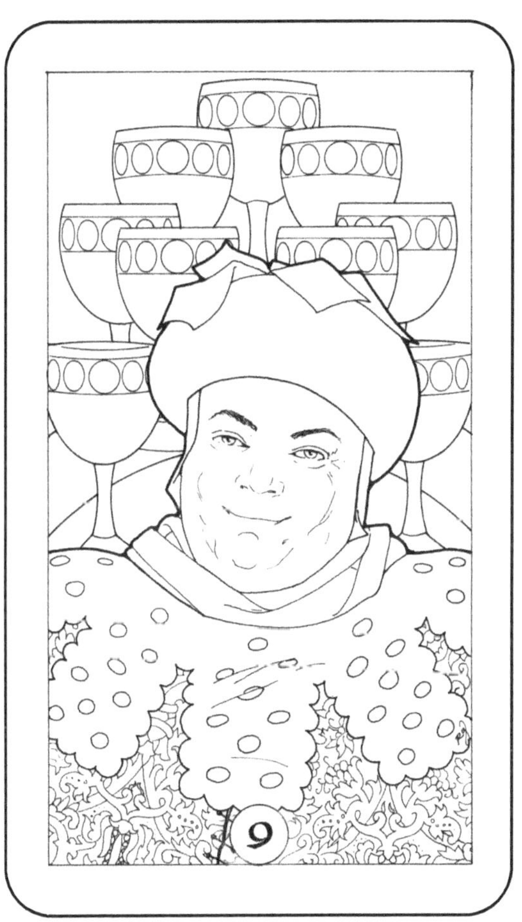

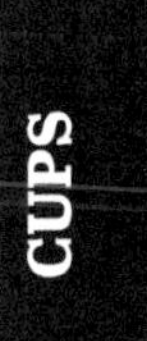

Notes:

Eight of Cups

Key - Enough of This!

Meaning - Abandonment of this phase of life, rejection of material things and a turning toward spiritual things. Disappointment in love. A search for new paths.

Reversed - A search for pleasure, hedonism, joy, new love, feasting. An abandonment of the responsibilities of life.

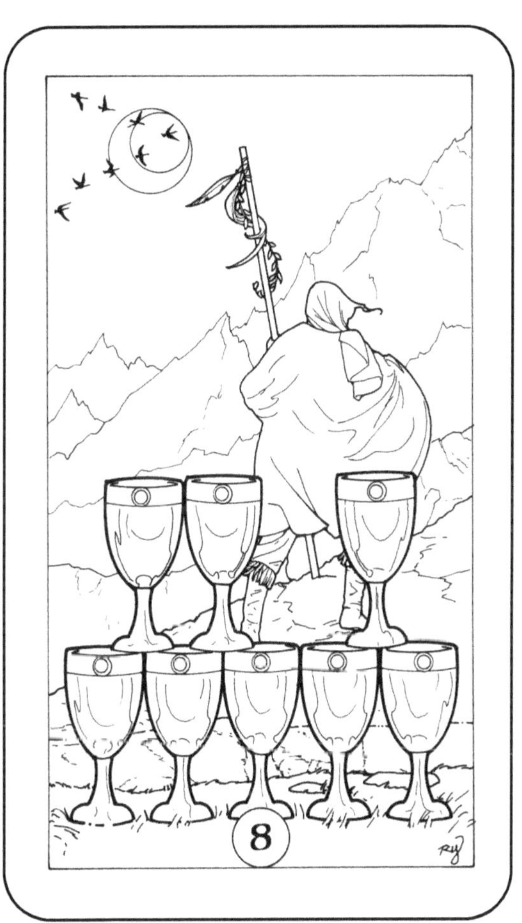

Notes:

Seven of Cups

Key - Dreams

Meaning - Overactive imagination. Inability to choose a single path or goal. Dreaming instead of acting. Head in the clouds. Illusion. A mystical experience, positive visualization. Victory over Death.

Reversed - Determination, strong will, action.

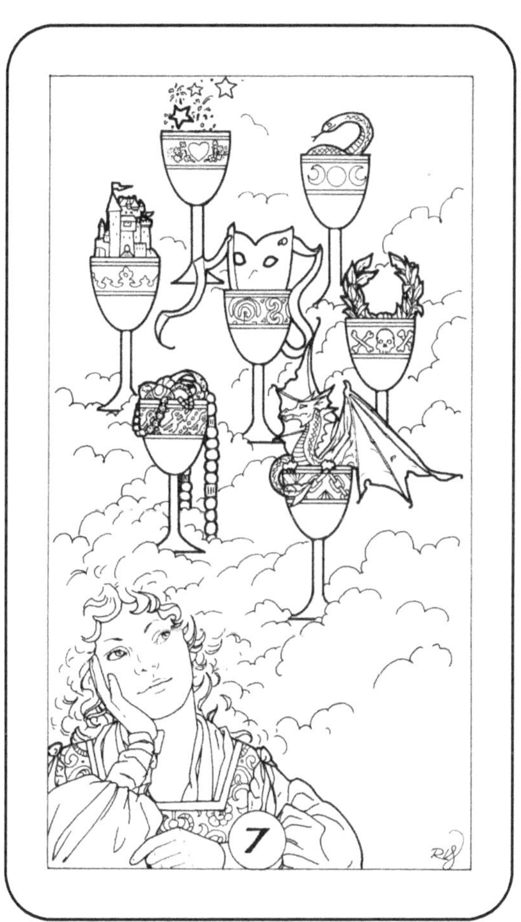

Notes:

Six of Cups

Key - Home and Childhood

Meaning - The past, memories, nostalgia, innocence, knight on a pillar, youthful idealism. Times which have passed by and vanished.

Reversed - The future, a renewal. Plans which may soon come true (or fail.)

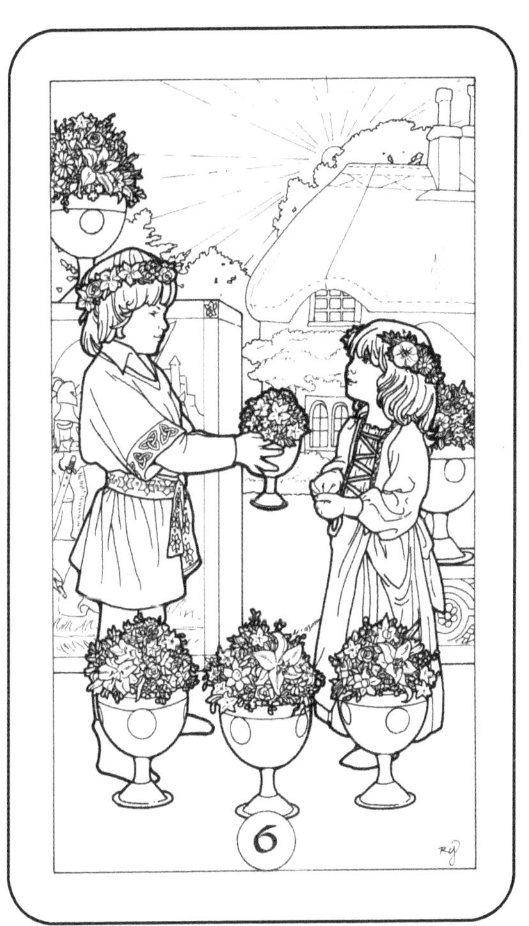

Notes:

Five of Cups

Key - Despair

Meaning - Sorrow, looks, disillusionment, bitterness, relationship ending (marriage, work, friendship.) Despite feelings, do not give up hope - look for the positive.

Reversed - Renewal, new alliances. The return of a lost one. Courage to overcome difficulties.

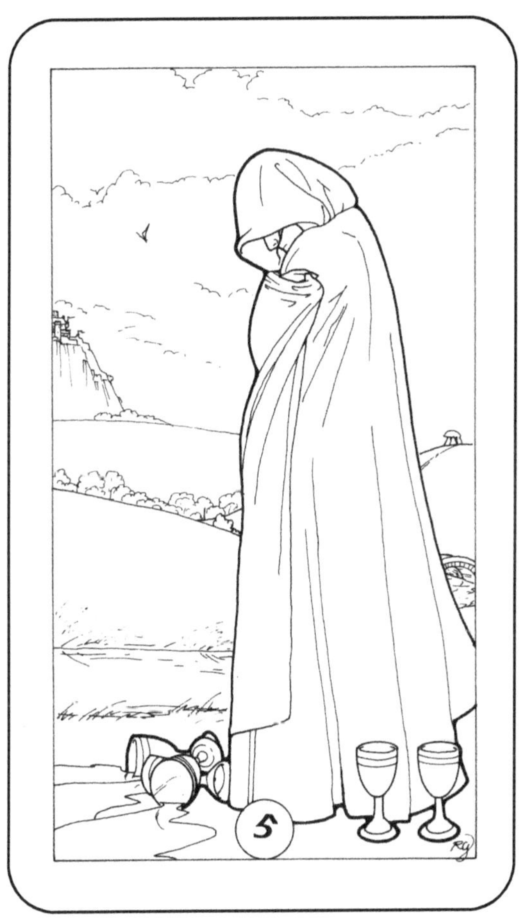

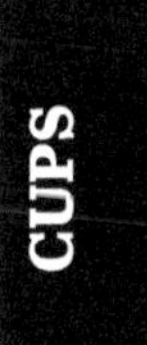

Notes:

Four of Cups

Key - Introspection and Discontent

Meaning - Discontentment with materialism. A time of introspection and contemplation. Start of self-awareness. Alternatively self-involvement. World-weariness. A search for understanding. Solitude. Disregarding offered gifts.

Reversed - New relationships. The beginning of action. New possibilities.

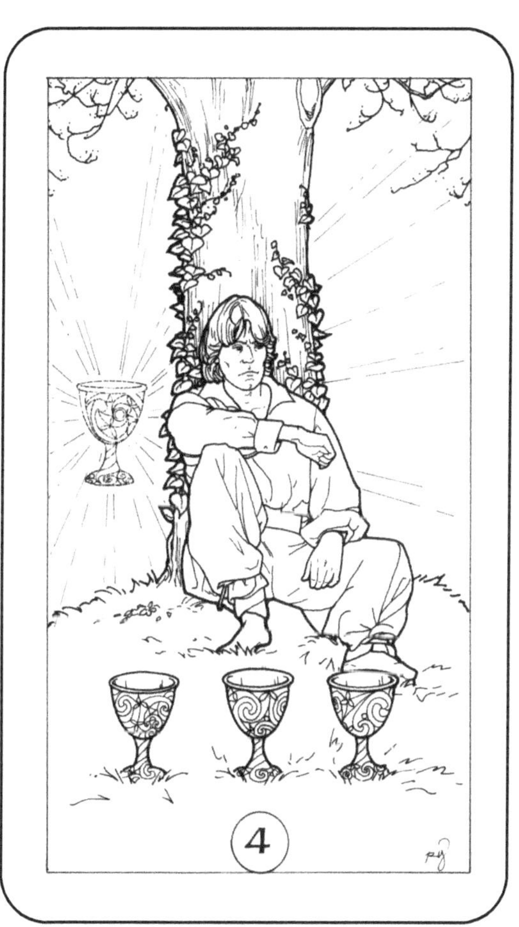

Notes:

Three of Cups

Key - Good Luck

Meaning - Good fortune, artistic ability, sensitivity. Perhaps a party is in store. Fulfillment, healing, harmony.

Reversed - Gluttony, overindulgence, delay. Abundance turns to lack, pleasure to pain. Talents are hidden or unappreciated.

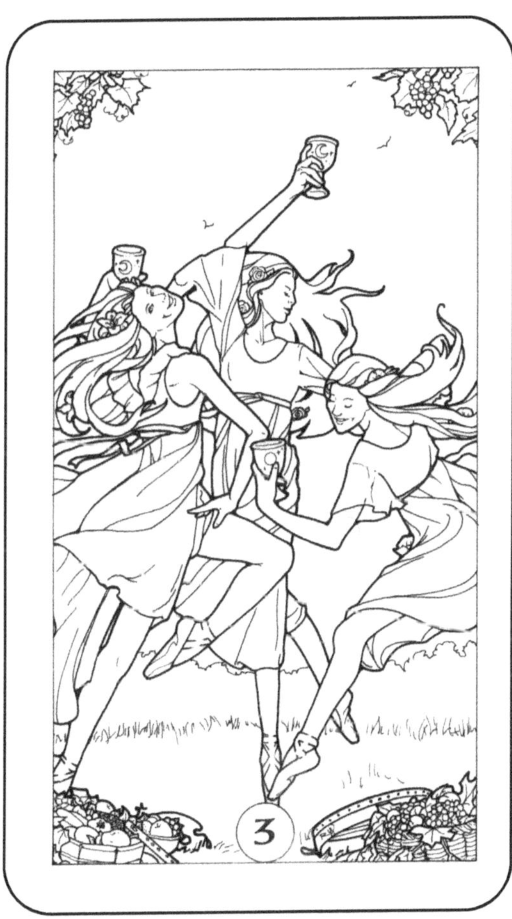

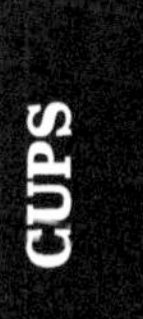

Notes:

Two of Cups

Key - Balance and Friendship

Meaning - Satisfying love, friendship, platonic love, a good partnership, harmony, cooperation. Two opposing forces bland and yield a glorious whole.

Reversed - Loss of balance, violent passion, love becoming hate, misunderstanding.

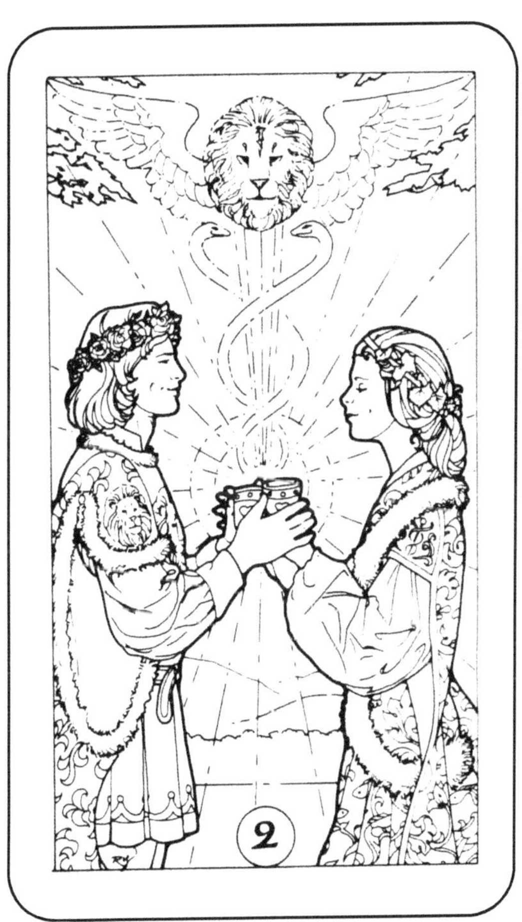

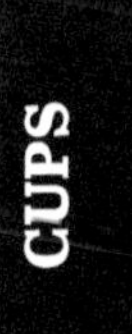

On the opposite page you'll find a pattern that is suitable for use on the back of the cards, if you are copying them onto card stock. Otherwise, you won't need it (although it might be fun to color!)

www.ingramcontent.com/pod-product-compliance
Lightning Source LLC
LaVergne TN
LVHW010619100826
845148LV00014B/3034